The Most
Beautiful English
美丽英文
BEAUTIFUL ENGLISH

久违的心灵之声，至深的人生哲理

The Most
Beautiful English

美丽英文

BEAUTIFUL ENGLISH

左手和右手的温差

Temperature Difference Between
Your Right and Left Hands

陈晓辉
一路开花 ◎ 主编

江苏凤凰美术出版社
全国百佳图书出版单位

图书在版编目（CIP）数据

左手和右手的温差：汉英对照/陈晓辉，一路开花
主编 . -- 南京：江苏凤凰美术出版社，2019.4
（美丽英文）
ISBN 978-7-5580-3398-8

Ⅰ . ①左… Ⅱ . ①陈… ②一… Ⅲ . ①英语—汉语—
对照读物 Ⅳ . ① H319.4

中国版本图书馆 CIP 数据核字（2017）第 290108 号

责任编辑　曹昌虹
封面设计　宋双成
责任监印　唐　虎

书　　名	左手和右手的温差：汉英对照
著　　者	陈晓辉　一路开花
出版发行	江苏凤凰美术出版社（南京市中央路 165 号　邮编：210009）
	北京凤凰千高原文化传播有限公司
出版社网址	http://www.jsmscbs.com.cn
印　　刷	北京飞达印刷有限责任公司
开　　本	710×1000mm　1/16
印　　张	14
版　　次	2019 年 4 月第 1 版　　2019 年 4 月第 1 次印刷
标准书号	ISBN 978-7-5580-3398-8
定　　价	29.00 元

营销部电话　010-64215835-801

江苏凤凰美术出版社图书凡印装错误可向承印厂调换　电话：010-64215835-801

目录
Contents

第一辑
弱者也是强者
Series 1   The Weakness is also The Strength

1

第二辑

锁不住的财富之门

Series 2   Unchained Door of Wealth

第三辑

抬起我们的头

Series 3 Raise Our Heads

第一辑 弱者也是强者

Series 1　The Weakness is also The Strength

　　没有任何成功比亲情更重要, 事业失败了可以重新再来, 一旦亲情丢失了, 生活将变得冰冷, 任何成功都不再有意义。因此无论什么时候, 我们都要把亲情放在事业之前, 因为亲情的关爱最值得珍惜。重视亲情, 不要自私, 勇于付出, 你也会拥有幸福的人生。

　　Success is never as important as family. You can start again if you fail, but once family is broken, life will become cold and dreary, and success will become meaningless. Whenever it is, family should be put prior to your business, because family care is the most precious and valuable. Attach great importance to family affection, never be selfish and be brave to make contribution, and you will live in happiness.

"吻"出精彩人生

文 / 倪西赟

人类要在竞争中求生存，更要奋斗。

——孙中山

7月15日，一位身穿蓝色旗袍校服的女生，在美国有线新闻网络(CNN)及各大媒体的镜头前，示范通过嘴唇阅读凸感盲文。她即是在今年全港中学文凭考试（即香港的"高考"）中，考得3科5++，2科5+的佳绩，成为第二届文凭试最耀眼的状元。可谁知道，镜头前这个一脸阳光，面带微笑，侃侃而谈的女孩，竟是一位患有失明、弱听和十指触感障碍的"三不感"人。

1993年，她出生于香港一个普通的家庭，她无论如何也想不到自己一出生，竟会有那么多的磨难在等着她。她出生几个月，就被发现视力有问题，父母抱着她去医院检查。医生告知她的父母她的神经严重萎缩，双目几乎失明，只能感觉到光和影，父母抱着她欲哭无泪。然而，磨难却接踵而来，在她四岁多的时候，父母发现她的手指尖也有触感缺陷，不能像一般失明学生那样双手触摸点字阅读。而到一年级，她听力也开始下降。这些不幸放在谁的身上，都将是不能承受的。

Kiss For A Wonderful Life

Human survive in competition.

——Sun Zhongshan

On July 15th, a girl in a blue Cheongsam showed how to read braille with lips before the lens of CNN and other mainstream media. As the top scorer in the second Hong Kong Diploma of Secondary Education Examination (similar to the university entrance examination in mainland China), she was the limelight that year with a high score of 5++ for three subjects and 5+ for the other two courses. Surprisingly, this optimistic girl, talking with confidence and smiles in front of the lens, is cursed with blindness, difficulties in hearing and finger touch.

She was born in 1993 in an ordinary family in Hong Kong. However, it was totally unexpected that she was born with so many difficulties waiting for her. Just several months after birth, she was diagnosed with visual impairment. When she was taken to hospital by her parents for medical examination, it was told that she could only feel the light and shadow as she was almost blind due to severe neuratrophy. Holding her in their arms, her parents were crying without tears. Nevertheless, hardships never come alone. When she was four, her parents found that she could not feel braille as other blind students did for reading, becaues of her finger touch disorder. At Grade 1, her hearing began to decline. These misfowrtune will not be borne by anyone.

一般的父母，看到自己的孩子有残疾，别说是读书，能够让孩子生活无忧也都觉得万幸了。然而她是幸运的，她的父亲是糕点师，母亲是全职家庭主妇，日子过得比较紧。但是，父母从没放弃这个"三感不全"的宝贝女儿，在生活上他们除了无微不至地照顾她，而且为了她能够及时读书、认字，将来有一技之长，成为一个有用的人，还让她按时上幼儿园，入读盲人学校。父母为了让她早些融入主流学校，在中一时便转往教学条件较好的英华女校。

在爱的围绕下她特别懂事，特别坚强，她在家里从不给父母添麻烦，在学校里遇到困难总是自己尝试解决。

一般视障人士，都是用手阅读盲文书，然而上天连她用手的能力都剥夺了，怎么办呢？她很是苦恼，但她从没有放弃。她不断尝试用身体的各个部位寻找最佳触点，终于有一天，她兴奋地发现，用双唇可以代替双手阅读。

每天，同学们都看到她把书放在嘴唇上，好像在与书时刻"亲吻"，从此，课堂上、校园里便多了一道独特的风景。

以唇"吻"书，看似浪漫，实则困难重重。刚开始，她一遍又一遍练习用嘴唇阅读，但不得要领。不得要领就不断地摸索，在她持之以恒的坚持下，终于熟练掌握了唇读的技巧。她用唇读点字每分钟大约读100个中文字，英文大概80到90个。

她虽然掌握了唇读的阅读方式，但相比之下，阅读同样的内容，她不仅比其他用手读书的盲人慢，更要比正常人多花两倍的时间。为此，在课堂前她要提前预习老师事先为她准备好的点字笔记，在课堂后，她几乎是除了吃饭、洗澡和睡觉外，其他的时间都用在阅读上。她认为，自己虽有听力障碍，但绝不能放宽对自己的要求。

在香港，有听力障碍的学生参加"高考"可获安排豁免中英文听力

When children are found with disabilities, parents in general would feel extremely lucky if their children can lead a carefree life, let alone going to schools. But she is blessed with fortune. Her father is a pastry cook while her mother is a housewife. Though not rich, they had never thought of giving up their precious daughter. In addition to taking great care of her, they supported her to go to kindergarten at the proper age and later in the School for the Blind so that she could get access to necessary education, and acquired certain competences and skills to become helpful to society. In order to help her better integrate into ordinary schools, they transferred her to Ying Hua Girl's School, a better middle school when she was at Grade 7.

She was quite considerate and strong surrounded by love and care. She never causes troubles for her parents at home and relies on herself to solve problems at school.

Those visually impaired people usually read braille with hands. But she was even deprived of her hands' sensing abilities. What else could she do? Though upset, she never gives up. Instead, she tried to use different parts of her body to find out the best touching point. Eventually, to her great delight, she could read with her lips as substitutes for hands.

Everyday, students would see her putting books on her lips as if "kissing" them all the time, developing into a unique view in class and at school.

It seems romantic to "kiss" books with lips. But actually, this process is filled with difficulties. At first, she tried again and again to practice lip reading but failed to grasp the main points. However, she continued to practice. With perseverance, she eventually mastered the technique of lip reading. Through lip reading, she is able to read nearly 100 Chinese characters and 80 to 90 English words every minute. Despite the fact that she is proficient in lip reading, it takes much more time for her to read the same text compared with other blind people and twice the time when compared with ordinary people. In light of this, she had to preview the braille notes prepared for her by teachers before classes. Except the time spent on eating, showering and sleeping, she spent all the remaining time on reading. She thought that there was no reason to loosen up because of hearing disorder.

In Hong Kong, students with hearing disorder will gain exemptions

的考试，这对她来说是一个特殊的"待遇"。但她考虑再三，毅然放弃享受这样的待遇，因为她知道，应该凭自己的能力去闯关，无论考出来的成绩怎么样，都要勇敢面对现实。如果这次选择逃避，那么这个困难永远没法克服了。

在考英国文学时她共花了 8 小时作答，中国文学则长达 10 小时，而一般考生只需要共 6 小时。因此，她付出了比常人多一倍的体力和努力，终于以优异的成绩被香港中文大学翻译系录取。她，就是香港励志少女曾芷君。

曾芷君的故事感动了很多人，香港特别行政区行政长官梁振英在网上发表《为了我们的未来》文章中特地赞扬了她"意志过人"，诗人半纳在献给曾芷君的诗中赞美她的少女之吻无数次地献给书本，连骄傲的蜜蜂、蝴蝶都自惭形秽……

"人生纵然充满荆棘，我依然无所畏惧。"面对种种困难，曾芷君依然很快乐。她认为，快乐的时光多不胜数，快乐总比烦恼多。

是的，磨难就像一座山，攀上这座山并把它踩在脚下，那么一切都是值得的，一切都是快乐的。

载于《意林·少年版》

智 慧 箴 言

> 每个人都有一段自己拼命的日子，那些日子，没有人告诉你怎么去做，也没有人陪伴你前行。但你得知道，自己不拼命，就没人救得了自己。身残志坚的曾芷君告诉我们：抵达成功不光是奋斗那么简单，还要有持之以恒的毅力。

for Chinese and English hearing tests when they participate in the university entrance exam. For her, this is a special treatment. With careful consideration, she decided to give up this treatment. She knew that she should pass the exam with her abilities. Whatever the final score was, she should face it. Evasion will only make it a permanent issue.

It took her 8 hours to finish the exam of English literature and as long as 10 hours for Chinese literature. In comparison, ordinary students will only need 6 hours to finish these two exams altogether. With unimaginably more energies and efforts made than ordinary people, she was finally admitted by the translation department of Chinese University of Hong Kong. She is Zeng Zhijun, an inspirational girl of Hong Kong.

Many people are touched by her story. Liang Zhenying, who is the Chief Executive of Hong Kong, once accredited her as with "exceptional willingness" in an online article entitled *"For Our Future"*. Moreover, Poet Ban'na praised her in the poem wrote for her by saying that the young girl's kiss is contributed to books for many times, even the proud bees and butterflies will feel ashamed.

"Life is full of thorns, but I will never be afraid of it." Confronted with so many difficulties, Zeng Zhijun still remains happy and optimistic. In her mind, happiness is countless and is much more than troubles.

It is true that hardship is like a mountain. But it is of a great value and enjoyment to climb up this mountain and stand at top of it.

Every individual has experienced days of endeavor and countless effort.During these days, nobody tells you how to do and no one has ever accompanied you to pass through. But you have to know that nobody but your efforts can save yourself. Disabled but persistent, Zeng Zhijun tells us: success is not as simple as only making efforts, it also needs perseverance.

劳丽诗：在心里养一朵菩提花

文 / 陈小蓝

当你的希望一个个落空，你也要坚定，要沉着！

——朗费罗

2014 年 9 月 19 日，阿里集团在纽交所上市，她以阿里集团上市敲钟人的身份出现在媒体面前，当媒体追问她是如何看待自己从奥运冠军到淘宝店主再到阿里上市敲钟人的华美蜕变的时候，她从容地回答说："这些得益于我在低谷期的磨砺和沉淀。"

她出生在广东湛江一个普通的家庭里。5 岁时，她的哥哥在业余体校学跳水，母亲则每天带着她接送哥哥去体校训练。她被跳水训练的弹网吸引住了，趁大家在跳台训练时，她一个人溜上了网。

她的大胆和良好的协调性令教练认定她是个跳水的好苗子，在教练的动员下，她加入了业余体校正式学跳水。由于训练的艰苦，她生了一场大病，病好之后她却打了退堂鼓。在母亲的劝导下她坚持下来了，这一坚持就是 4 年，也正是这 4 年光阴磨砺了她的意志和斗志。

9 岁那年，她参加湛江市运动会，比赛当天她发了高烧，母亲劝她退出比赛，可是一想到每一次的比赛机会都是来之不易的，她还是顶住

Lao Lishi: Keep a Bodhi Flower in Your Heart

Although your hope is lost, you must be firm and calm.

——Longfellow

On September 19, 2014, Ali Group listed in the NYSE, Lao Lishi as Ali group listed Bell people appear before the media. When the media asked her how she viewed her gorgeous metamorphoses from the Olympic Champions to Taobao shopkeeper and then to the listed Bell People, she calmly replied, these were the benefits of her honing and setting at a low point.

She was born in an ordinary family in Zhanjiang City, Guangdong province. At the age of 5, her brother was diving in a sports school, and her mother took her brother to the gym to train with her every day. She was attracted by the diving net, and she slipped into the net alone while everyone was training on the platform.

Her daring and good coordination have convinced her coach that she was a good diver, and she had joined the amateur sports school for formal diving. Because of the hard training, she developed a serious illness. After she was ill, she wanted to retreat. She persevered under her mother's persudation for four years, and it was the four years that honed her will and spirit.

When she was 9 years old, she took part in the Zhanjiang games. On the competition day, she had caught a high fever Her mother advised her

身体的不适坚持参加比赛。这一次的坚持，令她拿到跳水运动的第一个冠军。随后凭着坚强的意志和不服输的劲头，她从市队跳到省队、国家队，在人才济济的中国跳水界崭露头角。

接着，她夺得国际泳联跳水大奖赛西班牙站女子 10 米跳台单人冠军，加拿大站 10 米跳台冠军，美国站 10 米跳台双人冠军，全国跳水锦标赛女子 10 米跳台亚军，世界杯跳水赛女子 10 米跳台单人、双人冠军……那时的她可谓所向披靡，她一路向着奥运会的目标前进着。

正当她意气风发向奥运冲刺时，她的状态却一路下滑。她的身体频繁出现伤病，在一系列的世界大赛相继失手后，她内心失落、绝望、消沉。当领队告诉她：你缺的并不是实力，只要你做回自己时。她才恍然大悟，加强了大量的训练，终于恢复了自信。这一年，她终于站到了奥运会的跳台上，并获得了 10 米双人跳台金牌。

然而，所有的辉煌却在 17 岁这年戛然而止。她的身体状况越来越差，她想过退役，可是跳水运动曾是她的梦想，她不知道自己还能不能清晰地前往渴盼的目的地，自己渴盼的又是什么呢？当有人问她会什么，她可以回答"会跳水"，那么十年后呢，她还能理直气壮地回答吗？她的内心仿佛装满焦热之油，烈火一点，瞬间就能燃尽。

夏末初秋，空气有清凉的味道。她经过一座寺庙，一株巨大的粉红色的菩提花在眼前绽放，夕阳斜落在菩提花挺拔的苞叶和花瓣上，四周泛起金黄的光芒。一个中年女人经过菩提树下，惊异道："往年这树只能开 10 个花球，今年竟然开出了 30 多个花球，世事真是有多种可能啊。"

中年女人的话令她陷入了沉思，她一直以为梦想只能有一个，原来，只要有一颗向往的心，菩提花便会迸发出热情，绽放出令人意想不到的光芒。那么，梦想也能如菩提花开一般，拥有多变的光芒。这一

to quit the game, but she thought the every chance of the race is hard to come by, she still insisted on the competition uncomfortably. This time, she won the first championship in the diving sport. Then with a strong will and unyielding momentum, she jumped from the city team to the provincial team, the national team, and made a figure in the Chinese diving field which is full of talented athlete.

Then she won the FINA Diving Grand Prix Spanish station women 10-meter platform single-person champion, Canada station 10-meter platform champion, the United States station 10-meter platform double-person champion, the National Diving Championships women 10-meter platform runner-up, the World Cup diving tournament women 10-meter platform single-person, double-person champions, and so on. At that time, she was invincible, she was moving towards the goal of the Olympic Games.

When she was in the rush to the Olympics, her condition slipped. Her body was frequently injured, and missed in a series of World competitions, so she was lost, despaired and depressed. When the leader told her being herself rather than lack of the strength, it dawned on her that she had strengthened a lot of training and finally regained her self-confidence. This year, she stood on the Olympic platform and won the 10-meter double-person platform gold medal.

However, the entire splendor ended abruptly at the age of 17. Her body was getting worse and worse, so she wanted to retire, but diving was her dream and she did not know whether she can clearly go to the destination and she also did't know what she was eager for? When someone asked her what she was going to do, her answer was diving, and after ten years, could she still answer straightly? Her heart seemed filled with hot oil, and the fine could burn out in a moment.

The air has a cool taste in late summer to early autumn. She went through a temple and a giant pink bodhi blossomed in front of her eyes. Sunset slanted on the upright bracts and petals of Bodhi flowers, which were surrounded by golden glow. A middle-aged woman went through the bodhi and said with a great surprise, "In the past there were only 10 flower balls in this tree, this year had expelled more than 30 flower balls, and the world is a cot of possibilities."

刻，她的心顿时澄清如水。

她及时调整了自己的心态，选择了退役，并回中山大学继续本科学业。2011 年，她进入广东省青年志愿者行动指导中心任主任科员职务，从此踏上一个全新的公益领域。稳定的工作却带给她更多思考，她不喜欢过着一成不变的生活，这时，她提出辞职，成了一个没有组织的人。亲戚朋友对她的行为感到不解和惋惜，她却告诉自己静下来，听从心的指引，待沉淀之后去改变以后的人生。抛开荣誉的光环，踏踏实实做事，无所畏惧地迎接风雨和未来人生。

她坚决告别以前的光辉岁月开起了淘宝店，她挑选了自己一直钟爱的木雕和手串饰品项目，成为职业淘宝店主。她专注于店面装修、进货验收、找模特拍摄货品细节，经过几个月的努力，她的淘宝小店慢慢走向了正轨，她就是前跳水奥运冠军劳丽诗。

2014 年 9 月 19 号，阿里集团主要创始人马云邀请 8 名普通客户敲响开市钟，劳丽诗就是其中一个敲钟人，当记者问她为何会选择辞职开淘宝店时，她笑着说："真正的成功不是财富和地位，而是为了追求梦想放下身段，当我们感到迷惘时，在心灵深处种一株菩提树，积蓄养分，静静等待一朵属于自己的菩提花开。"

载于《新青年》

智慧箴言

面对梦想，我们真的需要去放下身段，去尽力呵护这份自己内心深处的念想。

The words of the middle-aged woman sunk her into deep thought, and she had always thought that dreams could only have one. However, as long as there was a yearning heart, the bodhi flower would burst out with enthusiasm and bloom an unexpected glow. Then the dream can also have the changeable light just like the Bodhi Blossom. This moment she was clear.

She adjusted herself in time and chose to retire, and went back to Zhongshan University to continue her undergraduate studies. In 2011, she became the director officer of the Guangdong Province Youth Volunteer Action Guidance Center, then she embarked on a new public welfare field. The steady work made her think, but she did not like to live a rut. Then she decided to resign. Relatives and friends of her were puzzled and sorry about her behavior, but she told herself to calm down, and followed heart of herself to change her life after the precipitation. Cast aside the aura of honor to work honestly and to greet the storm of the future life without fear.

She decided to bid farewell to the glory days of the past and set up Taobao shop. She picked up her favorite wood carving and hand jewelry, and became a professional Taobao shopkeeper. She focused on store decoration, stock and check, look for models and other details. After several months of efforts, her Taobao shop was on the right track. She is the former diving Olympic champion Lao Lishi.

On September 19, 2014, Ali Group's main founder Ma Yun invited 8 of ordinary customers ringing open Bell, and Lao Lishi is one of the bell men. When reporters asked why she chose to set up a Taobao shop, she smiled and said: "The real success is not wealth and status, but to pursue the dream by putting the minds down. When we feel confused, we should plant a bodhi tree deep in your heart, accumulate nutrients and wait for a bodhi flower that belongs to ourselves."

In the face of dream, we really need to put our minds down, to try to take care of your innermost thoughts.

光猪跑和泥巴大赛

文 / 宝谷

真者，精诚之至也，不精不诚，不能动人。

——庄子

近年来，越来越多的人开始跑步。他们因为不同的原因选择跑步，也因为跑步改变生活，北窗就是其中典型的一个。近几年来刚兴起的"光猪跑"和泥巴大赛，就是他发起的。

每年 2 月的最后一个周末，北京奥林匹克森林公园都会上演别具一格的"光猪跑"，2015 年 2 月末举办的已是第四届光猪跑。光猪跑全程 3.5 公里，气温零度以下，几十名跑步爱好者只穿着内衣裤进行"裸奔"。

2013 年 7 月在河北省张家口崇礼万龙滑雪场举行的首届泥巴大赛，又名"自虐山地障碍越野赛"。路线长达 13 公里，设置了泥潭、救赎、死亡行军、SM 尖叫、丛林野战、冰海沉浮、火线冲锋 7 大挑战性十足却又妙趣横生的环节。

北窗原名王以彬，光猪跑和泥巴大赛不是他一时兴起想要发起的，而是酝酿已久。北窗热衷于跑步，但他的热衷源于他大学时一次惨痛的

The Underwear Run and Mud Game

A sincere man should be as honest as possible. Without sincerity and honesty, it is impossible for him to move others.

——Zhuangzi

In recent years, more and more people have started running. One reason is that running can change people's life and Beichuang is the man who starts to run for this reason. Actually, he is the initiator of the "The Underwear Run" and Mud Came emerged recently.

During the last weeks of every February, a special "The Underwear Run" would took place in Beijing Olympic Forest Park. The end of the February of 2015 witnessed the Forth Naked Running held in China. With a total length of 3.5 kilometers, and the temperature below zero, tens of runners are running "naked" only in their underwear.

In July 2013, the first Mud Game, also known as "Self-Challenging Mountain Obstacle Cross Country" was held in Chongli Wanlong Ski Resort in Zhang Jiakou, Hebei Province. With a total length of 13 kilo meters, this competition was designed with 7 challenging but interesting sessions, including mire, salvation, death march, SM screaming, Jungle Battle, Driftage on Icy Sea, and Firing Line Rushing.

Rather than an instant idea, Wang Yibin, identified as Beichuang, had contemplated initiating the The Underwear Run and Mud Game for a long time. His passion about running can be traced back to a bitter experience in

经历。

上大学之前，北窗是个特别好胜的人，凡事都要争第一。考上香港大学之后，他依然争强好胜，有次北窗代表他的宿舍去参加港大的跑步比赛。比赛那天，他穿了一身新买的炫酷跑步装备，因为事先没试穿过，北窗很快在跑步过程中发现这身装备问题多多：鞋磨破了脚、袜子不透气、裤子太紧……于是还没跑到一半他就跑不下去了。他看见操场边有个小侧门，连忙像逃兵一样跑出去了。

北窗灰溜溜地回到自己的宿舍，感慨万分：一个人在准备一件重要的事情时，一点闪失、一点大意、一点骄傲都不能有，否则就会失败……跑步伤了北窗一次心，此后他很长一段时间都不再跑步。

有天他心情特别糟糕，在走廊来回踱步，楼道里，不知哪个宿舍开着门播放 Beyond 的那首《海阔天空》。北窗听得特别有感觉，他突然发现，自己的跑鞋早已被束之高阁。于是他取下跑鞋穿上就出去跑步了，跑着跑着他迷路了，跑到山上的森林中去了。但他没有惊慌，反而意外发现不在操场的跑步很自由。

不追求目标不追求成绩，跑步就是为了让汗水洗去不爽的感觉，北窗因此爱上了这项看似枯燥的机械运动。他几乎跑遍了各大马拉松赛事，曾跑步上雪山，海拔高达 4000 米；也曾跑步闯冰湖，超低气温零下 30 度。

在他看来跑步永远是移步换景的，并且规则少，可以跑各种地形、各种天气，甚至各种海拔。北窗想与更多人分享这样的感受，于是先后发起了光猪跑和泥巴大赛。

光猪跑时，北窗定了一个很有意思的规矩：谁第一个跑到终点，一定要受罚。原来，北窗定义，光猪跑就是一种放下的感觉。他说："你什么时候不再顾及别人的眼光，不再拿别人的价值观判断自己，敢于把

his university.

Before going to university, Beichuang was an emulative person who demanded himself to excel in everything he did. He was still competitive when he came to the University of Hong Kong, Once he represented his dorm to participate in the running race of HKU. On the day of competition, he wore new and fascinating running apparel. As he had never tried it on, no later than the beginning did he find the problems of his apparel: the shoes were rubbing his feet, the socks stifled his feet, and the trousers were too tight...As a result, he gave up halfway through the race. When noticing a small side door at the playground, he ran away like a deserter.

Beichuang returned to his dorm through the "back door" and filled with deep emotions: when one is preparing for something important, he will fail if there are any mishaps, carelessness and arrogance. This race was so heart-broken that Beichuang refused to run for a very long time.

One day, he walked back and forth in the passage in a bad mood. A dorm with its door opened was playing a song called *Unrestrained and Far-reaching* by Beyond. Deeply touched by the song, he suddenly realized that he had gone so long without using his running shoes. Therefore, he decided to put them on for running. When he was running, he lost his way and ran to the forest in the mountain. Without panic, he suddenly found that running in places other than playground was carefree and liberated instead.

It is not the pursuit of a goal or achievement but the feeling to wash away your bad mood with your sweat that delivers the true essence of running. Deeply attached to this seemingly boring mechanical movement, Beichuang has participated in almost every marathon. Once, he even ran on a snow mountain with an elevation of 4,000 meters and also ran across an icy lake on an extremely cold day when it was 30 Celsius degree below zero.

According to him, running offers changing scenes through movement of steps. With little rules, it is not restricted to landforms, weathers and even altitudes. In order to share this feeling with others, Beichuang successively launched the Naked Running and Mud Competition.

Beichuang made an interesting rule to naked running. The first to the finishing line will be punished. Because, as Beichuang put it, naked

自己脱光，敢于把自己真实的一面展现给别人，你就是光猪跑的胜利者。"因此，他鼓励大家结伴一起跑，放下自己，放下名次，一起追求自由的脚步。

泥巴大赛源于美国著名的比赛"斯巴达赛跑"，北窗把它带入国内，并给其定了口号——只为真的汉子，为的就是让人们去体验大自然的野性。

他将第一个障碍设置为大泥潭也别有用意。"当你跳入又脏又浑的泥潭之后，你就放开了，不再顾及平常害怕的东西。人的恐惧的本质，其实就是未知。很多你想象中的困难，当你真的去迎头痛击时，你会发现根本没那么难、没那么可怕。"

北窗说他最喜欢美国作者克里斯托弗·麦克杜格尔著作的《天生就会跑》里的一句话："跑步不是为了更快，而是为了无所畏惧。"北窗把这句话理解为：一个人无所畏惧了，就能放下很多东西，需求就变得很少。那时候，他就变得真正自由。

载于《知识窗》

智 慧 箴 言

　　人生的大部分时间是受到规则或者世俗眼光的制约的，所以欠缺自由和自我。生命中应该多些这样的时刻，抛开世俗的观念，做最真的自己。

running is a symbol of letting go. He said, only when you stop caring about others' judgements and stop judging yourself with others' value and when you brave yourself to run naked and show the true you to others, can you be the winner of the race. So he encouraged people to run shoulder by shoulder, put down themselves and the ranking, and set out for freedom.

Mud Game is originated from a famous US race called "Spartan Race". Beichuang brought it back to China and made a slogan for it—for the real man so that people can experience the wildness of nature.

It is for something special to use big mire as the first barricade. "When you jump into the dirty mire, you will totally release yourself without considering what you are afraid of. The essence of human fear is unknowingness. Many perceived hardships are actually not difficult and frightening at all when you wrestle with them directly."

Beichuang mentioned one of his favorite statements made by the US writer Christopher McDougall in his book *Born to Run* that: "Running is not for faster, but for fearless." He interpreted it as when one is fearless, he can release himself and reduce his secular needs. At that time, he will become truly free.

For most of our life, we are restricted to rules and secular perspectives that result in our lack of freedom and ego. In our life, we should find more chances to get rid of conventional views to stay true to ourselves.

优势有时会成为负担

文 / 宝谷

名誉过高，实在是一个沉重的负担。

——福尔特

每逢大学毕业季，大学生们就忙着找工作。大多数人认为，有优势的能最先找到工作，但实际上，往往是那些没有优势的学生最先找到工作。

一位心理学家举例解析了这一奇怪的现象。

大草原上分旱季和雨季。雨季过后，旱季来临，到处干旱，草木枯死，动物渴死。在旱季来临之前，动物们都要逃跑，以躲避旱灾，不被渴死。那么，在逃跑的时候，是跑得快的动物渴死的多，还是跑得慢的动物渴死的多？

答案是：跑快的动物渴死的多。原因很简单：跑得慢的动物风险意识较强。比如乌龟，它会想：我走得这么慢，下个月旱灾就来了，这个月得赶紧收拾东西先走。于是，跑得慢的动物都提前走了。而跑得快的动物，比如兔子，在旱季快要到来之前，可能还一边晒着太阳一边啃着胡萝卜想："我的速度这么快，明天旱灾来临，今天跑都来得及。"兔

Advantages Can Sometimes become A Burden

Too much fame is a heavy burden.

—— Faltere

During the senior year of graduates university, they are always busy finding a job. From the perspective of most people, it is easier for advantageous students to find a job. But actually, those who are employed first are usually the ones without advantages.

A psychologist used an example to explain this paradoxical phenomenon.

There is dry season and rainy season on the prairies. When the dry season comes after the monsoon, drought is everywhere so that plants and animals are dying of thirst. Before the dry season, animals will run away so as to survive the drought and avoid thirst to death. So, whether the fast animals die of thirst, or the slow animals die of thirst?

The answer is that: animals run fast are more die of thirst. The reason is simple: those run slowly have greater sence of risk. For instance, a turtle would think: moving at such a slow pace, I have to leave this month before the drought comes next month. Therefore, animals move slowly are left in advance. In comparison, animals running fast, such as rabbits, may still enjoy the sunshine while eating a carrot before a drought, they are thinking, "I can leave today before the drought comes tomorrow as I can run quickly." Thinking there is always enough time, rabbits will postpone

21

子觉得自己有足够的应变时间，于是今天推明天，明天推后天，结果旱灾真的来临时它再想跑已经晚了。

　　心理学家的解析告诉我们一个道理：很多时候，优势会成为我们的负担，资源会成为我们的盲点。因此当我们占据优势时，更要特别注意防范风险。

载于《哲思》

智 慧 箴 言

　　生于忧患，死于安乐。每个人都应该有居安思危的意识，不是为了躲避危险，而是在危险来临的时候，我们可以从容应对。

their actions to tomorrow and then the day after tomorrow until it is late to run when drought comes.

The psychologist reveals a truth: for many times, advantages will become our burden and resources may change into blind spots. When we take advantage, we have to pay special attention to risks.

He that lives in sorrow,dies in happiness. Everyone should have a sense of vigilance, not to avoid danger, but to deal with it at ease when it comes.

带刺的长椅

文 / 睿雪

> 在太空时代，最重要的空间是存在于耳朵与耳朵之间。
>
> ——托马斯 J·巴楼

德国柏林有个公园很特别：里面有十几条吸引眼球的长椅，其表面布满了四厘米长的锥形钢刺。许多游客说这样的椅子中看不中坐，唯有当地的居民知道，这十几条长椅是最人性化的设计。

长椅的设计者是公园管理员法比安·布伦森，布伦森年轻时是名设计师，退休后来公园做管理员。他经常能看到这样的场景：一条长椅上坐着两个人，左边的人看着手机傻笑，右边的人则盯着手机狂喊"加油"。他们顶多相距 50 厘米，可内心世界却像隔了十万八千里，你聊你的天，我看我的球赛，互不干扰。

这让布伦森意识到，人和人之间最遥远的距离不是生与死，而是两个人紧挨着，却各自关注着另一个世界。他真想撤掉公园里所有的长椅，让人们没地方坐下来看手机。可是，那样只会招来两个结果，人们要么不断抱怨，要么直接走人，回家继续摆弄手机。

Barbed Bench

In the space age, the most important space is between the ear and ear.

——Thomas J. Barrow

There is a unique park in Berlin where there are over a dozen of eye-catching benches that their surfaces are covered with four-centimeter-long tapered steel spike. Many tourists comment that these benches cannot be seated on. But only the local residents understand that these benches are the most humane design.

The designer of these benches is the park's administrator Fabien Brunson. He used to be a designer when he was young and worked as the administrator after retirement. He always sees that: when there are two people seating on the bench, the one on the left is giggling at the mobile phone while the other on the right is staring at the phone, shouting "come on". There is at most 50 centimeter between their bodies but hundreds and thousands of miles between their minds. I am chatting with others and you are watching your game: there is no interaction or exchange between us.

This reminded Brunson of that the farthest distance between people is not life and death, but when two people are next to each other, they are concerned only with another world. How much he wishes that he could remove all the benches in the park so that there will be no place for people to sit down playing their phones. This, however, can only lead to two outcomes: one is continual complaint and the other is people's leaving directly back home, continuing fiddling with phones.

经过一番思考，布伦森最终向当地政府申请将公园的长椅改成"锥刺股"款式。得到允许后，他先设计出一个投币盒和一个连接着十几根钢刺的线路板。然后，在每条长椅表面上均匀地钻上十几个孔洞，孔洞里安装的正是那十几根钢刺。平时，这些钢刺都是冒出的状态，当人们往投币盒投入50欧分后，钢刺缩回到椅子中，人们就可以坐下休息。

钢刺缩回的时间是十分钟，时间一到，椅子就会发出尖锐的警告声，十几秒后，钢刺又会重新冒出来。对于散步疲惫的人们来说，十分钟的休息已经足够；而对于玩手机的人来说，十分钟一晃就过，能有效起到"扫兴"的作用。

每条长椅都有一条相同的标语：请别让每天在此走路的距离小于手指滑动屏幕的距离。

带刺的长椅使用一段时间后，居民们这样评价：长椅虽有些"邪恶"，但让我们觉悟——试着放下手机，多和家人、朋友甚至陌生人面对面地交流。

载于《时代文摘》

智 慧 箴 言

电子产品的出现，的确方便了人们的生活，可是在另一方面，却也影响了人们的生活。缺乏交流缺乏沟通，几乎成了全社会的通病了。

With considerations, he applies to the local government to cover the benches with spikes. When this decision is approved, he firstly designed a coin box and a circuit board connected with more than a dozen of steel thorns. Then, over a dozen holes are evenly drilled on the bench and the steel thorns are put in them. Usually, these thorns are emitted, but when people put 50 Euro cents into the coin box, the thorns will stab back so that people can sit down for a break.

The steel thorns will be contracted for ten minutes later, when it will give alarm for about ten seconds. After that, they will spring out again. Ten minutes is enough for people tired of walking, but for those playing mobile phone, ten minutes passed by. Therefore, it can suppress their interest in mobile phones.

There is one slogan on each bench: please walk more and play your mobile phone less.

After being used for a period of time, these benches with thorns are accredited by local residents, though somewhat "evil", they have enabled us to think—putting down the mobile phones to spare more time for face-to-face communication with families, friends or even strangers.

No doubt that the electronics have offered convenience for our life, but it has also impacted our life as well. The lack of communication has become an almost universal disease.

周星驰的第一场戏

文 / 朱国勇

世界上的一切光荣和骄傲，都来自母亲。

——高尔基

  母亲与父亲离异那一年，周星驰才七岁，他和姐姐周文姬、妹妹周星霞一同判给了母亲凌宝儿。在 1968 年的香港，一个女人带着三个孩子讨生活，其艰难可想而知。为了维持生活，凌宝儿一个人打了两份工。令她欣慰的是，孩子们都特别乖巧懂事，尤其是周星驰，成绩十分优秀，最得凌宝儿钟爱。

  只有一件事，让凌宝儿烦心。

  三个孩子都正是长身体的时候，所以不管多么困难，每个星期，凌宝儿都要称点肉或买条鱼给孩子们加餐。或许是平时太娇惯了，或许是难得吃上一回鱼肉，菜一上桌，周星驰就把菜端到自己的碗边，专拣好的吃。姐姐妹妹却懂事得很，从不和他争。但是周星驰的饭量很小，吃了两块就吃不下去了。然后，他就开始胡闹，还要捡两块，放到嘴里嚼两下，再吐到碟子里。他嚼过了的，姐姐妹妹哪还肯吃啊！为了不浪费，凌宝儿只好自己吃。

The First Role Zhou Xingchi Played

All the glory and pride of the world are from the mother.

——Gorky

It was at the age of 7 when Zhou Xingchi's parents got divorced. Zhou Wenji, Zhou XingXia and he, awarded to his mother Ling Baoer. How hard it was to live with three children for a single mother in Hong Kong in 1968. Ling Boer had two jobs to meet ends meet. To her great delight, her children were clever and well behaved. In particular, Zhou Xingchi, excelled in academic studies, was her favorite child.

But there was one particular thing that bothered Ling Boer.

Since the three children were growing up, no matter how tight the budget was, Ling Baoer would buy some meat or to increase their nutrition intake. It may be the fact that Zhou Xingchi was much too spoiled in days, when the fish or meat was offered, he would put the dishes in front of him, only eating the delicious food. In comparison, her sisters were quite considerate and never scrambled with him for food. Zhou Xingchi ate so little that he could not eat too much. Then he began to make mischief, put two pieces of meat in it, and chew it up and spit it into the saucer. How could his sisters eat the chewed meat! In order not to waste, Ling Boer had to eat by herself.

为这事，凌宝儿没少批评周星驰，但是一点作用都没有。好在周星驰别的方面表现都很好，日子久了，凌宝儿就随他去了。小孩子嘛，哪有不顽皮的呢？

可是有一次，凌宝儿真的生气了，狠狠地教训了周星驰一顿。

那一次，凌宝儿两个月没发工资了，好不容易从娘家弄来了一些钱，买了几只鸡腿，烧得金黄喷香。菜刚上桌，周星驰就小猴儿似的爬上桌，抓起一只鸡腿就啃，还冲着姐姐妹妹做鬼脸。一不小心，手一滑，鸡腿掉地上了，沾满了尘土，落在一摊鸡屎旁边。

凌宝儿又是生气又是心疼，买这几只鸡腿容易吗？再想想周星驰平时的顽皮表现，凌宝儿决定这次要好好教训他。她取过一根桑树条，狠狠地抽了周星驰十几下："让你顽皮，让你不知珍惜？"直到周文姬与周星霞扑过来把周星驰护在身体下，凌宝儿才放下桑树条，搂着三个孩子抱头痛哭。

哭了好一会儿，才又开始吃饭。凌宝儿把鸡腿捡了起来，舍不得扔，就用开水冲洗一下，自己吃了。

那天晚上，凌宝儿抚着周星驰身上的伤痕："还疼吗？"

"不疼了。"

"下次还调皮吗？"

黑暗中，周星驰的眼睛十分明亮，他"嘻嘻"地笑着："睡吧，妈，我明天还要上课呢。"

2001年，周星驰、凌宝儿做客凤凰卫视时，又说起了这件往事。

"是的，那时他可是真顽皮啊，全不知道这饭菜来得多不容易，一点也不珍惜。"凌宝儿笑容慈祥。

"不，妈妈，我懂得珍惜。"周星驰接过话茬儿，声音开始哽咽，"您想想，我要是不把鸡腿弄到地上，您会舍得吃吗？那几年里，有什

She criticized him for many times for this reason, but it isn't of any use. Considering his excellent performance in other respects, Ling Baoer just let him do that after a long period of time. After all, kids are naughty sometimes.

But one day, Ling Baoer was so annoyed that she gave him a good lesson.

Lin Baoer did not get paid for two months. Finally getting some money from her parents, she bought several drumsticks and cooked them deliciously. When the dish was put on the table, Zhou Xingchi climbed on the table like a monkey and got a drumstick. While eating, he made funny faces to his sisters. Accidentally, the drumstick slipped his hand and dropped on the ground covered with dirt just beside a pool of chicken shit.

Ling Baoer was annoyed and distressed, as drumstick was a luxury for her family. In light of his mischievous behavior, she decided to give him a lesson. She beat him with a mulberry branch, scolding, "how could you be mischievous, and how could you have no idea of cherishing?" It was not until her two daughters came at her to protect Zhou Xingchi and the put down the branch and hugged the three children and cried bitterly.

Crying for a while, they began to have their meals. Picking up the drumstick, Ling Baoer was so reluctant to throw it away, so she washed it with boiling water and ate it.

That evening, touching the scar on his body，she asked, "is that still hurt?"

"Not any more."

"Will you act mischievously again?"

Zhou Xingchi's eyes were sparkling in darkness, giggling, he said, "It's time for sleep mom. I have classes tomorrow."

In 2001, when they were invited by Phoenix Satellite Television, Zhou Xingchi and Ling Baoer mentioned it again.

"Yes, he was so naughty that he had no idea how hard it was to earn the food. He didn't know how to cherish." Ling Baoer kindly smiled.

"No, mom. I know how to cherish." Zhou Xingchi responded with his voice choked with tears, "have you ever thought that if I did not drop

么好吃的，您全给了我们姐弟三人，您成天就只吃咸菜，于是我们才想出这个办法，我把几块肉嚼得不像样后，我们就有借口不吃了。只有这样，您才会吃啊！"

听着这话，凌宝儿情绪变得激动起来："其实，我早该想到，你样样乖巧懂事，怎么偏偏在吃饭这方面这么顽皮呢?"凌宝儿哽咽着掏出手帕擦眼睛。

周星驰挂着两行泪水满面微笑，在亿万电视观众面前，这对母子抱在了一起。无数的观众也在这一刻，流下泪来。

虽然周星驰演戏无数，精品众多，但是我要说，他最好的戏，是在他七岁那年，演绎的那份血浓于水、骨肉连心的挚爱亲情，唯一的观众，是他的母亲。

载于《读者》

智 慧 箴 言

没有无私的、自我牺牲的母爱的帮助，孩子的心灵将是一片荒漠。有这样一个忘我牺牲的模范母亲，又怎能不做一个好孩子呢?

the drumstick on the ground, would you be willing to eat? In those years, you gave everything delicious to us and treated yourself only with pickles every day! So, we came up with this idea that if I chewed the meat, we had excuses for not eating it. Only in this way could you eat it!"

Hearing this, Ling Baoer became thrilled, "I should have known it. How could such a considerate and smart kid act so mischievously only during the meals!" She took out her handkerchief to wipe the tears.

Zhou Xingchi smiled with tears on his face. In front of tens of millions of audience in front of the TV, the mother and the son embraced each other. At this moment, countless audience burst into tears.

Though he played many roles, many of which are quite impressive, but what I want to say is that the best role he has ever played was at the age of 7 when he showed how family love was like blood thicker than water and the only audience was his mother.

Without the help of selfness and sacrificial from mother's love, the child's heart will be a desert. How could he grew up into someone evil with such a sacrificial mother as a model.

把眼泪变成钻石

文 / 佳山

理想的路总是为有信心的人预备的。

——谚语

一个女孩，1976 年出生于美国的宾夕法尼亚州的艾伦敦市，父亲是从爱尔兰移民来的泥瓦匠，母亲是一个售货员。她出生时，小腿就没有长腓骨，已完全丧失了行走的功能。1 岁生日那天，她被截掉了膝盖以下的小腿。女孩刚懂事时，母亲就对她说："孩子，你生来就是为了历经不平凡之事的，悲伤没有用，你要把眼泪变成钻石。"

女孩记住了母亲的话，一扫悲悲切切的阴霾，变得活泼开朗起来，充满了挑战和冒险精神。

然而，那时当地的诸多工厂纷纷倒闭，一场"美国梦"被残酷的现实击得粉碎。父母不能为她提供良好的教育环境，更别提时刻保护她不受外界侵害了。但是，父母却没有丝毫地娇惯她，而是让她和其他所有孩子一样去上学。

随着身体的发育，她的残肢必须进行相应的修整，为此，她总共接受了 5 次矫正手术。因为她长着棕色的头发，因为她跑得慢，因为人

Turning Tears Into Diamond

The ideal road is always prepared for those confident.

——Proverb

There was a girl born in 1976 in Allentown, Pennsylvania, the United States. Her father was a mason who emigrated from Ireland and her mother was a salesman. When she was born, she had no fibula, thus completely lost her walking abilities. When she was 1 year old, her legs below the knees were amputated. When she had sensibility, her mother told her, "Baby, you were born to experience an extraordinary life. There is no use to be sad. You have to turn your tears into diamonds."

The girl memorized what her mother said and prevented all her distress. She became optimistic, and was full of challenging and adventurous.

Unfortunately, many local factories were closed down at that time and the "American dream" was broken by the brutal reality. Her parents were unable to provide her with a good education environment, let alone protecting her from external damages. Instead coddling her, they educated and afforded her to go to school like other children.

As she grew up, the residual limbs had to be adjusted. Therefore, she experienced five corrective procedures. Children always teased her because she had brown hair, ran slowly and people looked at her strangely. In

们爱拿异样的眼光看待她，所以，孩子们总取笑她。为了释放精神上的压力和烦恼，她就泡一个热水澡，然后就是和两个小弟弟踢球或是去骑车。为了增强体力，她每周日起床后都要做104组"醒神操"。

上大学时付不起学费，她听说国防部在乔治敦大学开设了一项国际关系奖学金后，果断报了名，最终以优异的成绩通过考试。而且，她还有幸结识了一名优秀的田径教练 p 老师。那位老师对她说的第一句话就是："嗨，强壮的小姑娘！"这给了她巨大的鼓舞，使她眼前一片光明，老师开始教她练跑步和跳远。

有一次她参加学校的田径赛 100 米跑，跑到一半，她的义肢突然掉了，她重重地摔倒了。所有的人都惊诧不已地望着她，她看了看老师，老师纹丝不动，只是挥了挥手，叫她装上义肢再跑。后来，老师对她说："人生也如赛场，停顿只有失败。"从此以后，女孩更加顽强，不屈不挠。

后来，她第一次参加全国田径赛就打破了 100 米跑国家纪录，这也点燃了她征战亚特兰大残奥会的渴望。果然，1996 年，20 岁的她，用碳纤维特制的义肢刷新了两项世界纪录：女子 100 米跑和跳远，尽管，她每跑一步都要花费正常人四倍的力气。她一下子成了美国人的骄傲和楷模，也激励了成千上万美国人的梦想。她受邀出席各种重大场合，为女子体育基金奔走呼号，登上各类杂志封面。

1999 年，英国服装设计大师亚历山大·麦坤邀请她做服装模特。T 台上，她那高高的木质义肢像双靴子一样，她又显得那样从容不迫，仪态万方，婀娜多姿，令人赞叹不已。走秀后，很多人到后台向她祝贺。

如今，她已是名扬世界的残疾模特，她叫艾米·穆林斯。

order to release her psychological pressure and troubles, she always played football or biking with two younger brothers after taking a shower. To keep strength, she 104 sets of "Waking Up Calisthenics" when she got up every Sunday.

As she was unable to afford her university, when she informed the international relations scholarship in Georgetown University granted by Department of Defense, so she applied for it immediately and was finally admitted due to her outstanding performance. In addition, she had a pleasure to meet a good track coach. The first sentence the coach talked to her was "Ah, such a strong young girl!" which greatly inspired and created hope for her. Then, the coach began to teach her run and long jump.

One day, when she took part in the 100-meter track and field race of school, her artificial limb dropped after she finished half of the race. Then, she fell heavily on the ground. Everyone looked at her with great surprise. She looked at her coach who, however, did not move but just waved his hands, telling her to put on her artificial limb and keep on running.

Later on, she broke the national record of 100m sprint in the first time she took part in national track and field race, which ignited her desire for the Atlantic Paralympics. As expected, in 1996, the girl, in her twenties, refreshed two world records with carbon fiber-made prostheses: women's 100 meters and long jump. Though she had to make four times as much as the efforts than an ordinary people to run every step, she became the pride and model of American people and inspired the dreams of tens of thousands of American people. She was invited to attend many important events, she appealed for women's sports funds and became the cover figure of various magazines.

In 1999,Britsh fashion designer Alexander McQueen invited her as model. On the T stage, her high wooden prostheses liked a pair of boots but she seemed so calm, graceful, elegant and amazed. Many came to the backstage to congratulate her after the show.

Today, she is a well-renowned model of disability worldwide. Her name is Amy Mullins.

现在，艾米又荣登全球知名化妆品品牌欧莱雅形象大使的宝座。有人说，艾米是一出戏，一个传奇。艾米说："真正的残疾是被击败的灵魂。"只要灵魂不败，就有成功的希望，就能把眼泪变成钻石，活出光辉灿烂的自己。

载于《知识窗》

智慧箴言

　　每一个残缺的人都是让上帝咬过一口的苹果，不论身体如何，至少灵魂是丰满的。所以，永远不要放弃自己。

Now, Amy has becomes the image ambassador of the world's leading cosmetic brand L'Oreal. Some said that Amy is a play and a legend. Amy said, "The real disability is a defeated soul." There is a hope for success as long as the soul is undefeated. You can turn your tears into diamonds and live a brilliant self.

Every disabled person is an apple once bit by God. Regardless of his body, his soul is complete. So, never give up yourself.

强者自救，圣者渡人

文 / 随风

穷且益坚，不坠青云之志。

——王勃

他出生在丹麦比隆，20世纪30年代初，已经41岁的他遇到了人生中最大的坎儿。

他是一个木匠，凭着出色精湛的木工技艺开了一家木制加工厂，生意还算不错。但是1932年的经济大萧条冲击到了这个小镇，所有的手工艺人都接不到订单，他也辞掉了最后的一名工人。

紧接着，妻子一场大病后离开人世，留下他和四个孩子在偌大的木制厂里相依为命，最小的孩子6岁，最大的孩子15岁。面对厄运，他犹豫不决：如果不能重新再来，那就找一份工作来做。

一个偶然的机会，他遇到了在工业协会上班的好友杜楠特，杜楠特告诉他："你的手艺那么好，一定不要放弃这个老本行，可以制作那些花钱不多，家庭必备的木制家用小产品啊！"

他听后觉得还不错，回到家里，几个孩子正拿着玩具做游戏，他突然意识到自己的主攻产品应该是玩具，他心想："玩是孩子的天性，

A strong man saves himself and a great man saves another

Impoverishment will make you stronger and never succumb to others.

——Wang Bo

He was born in a small village called Billund, Denmark. At the beginning of 1930s, he encountered the greatest barrier in his life when he was 41.

As a carpenter with a excellent woodworking skill, he opened a wooden processing factory which business was fairly well. However, the great depression hitting the town in 1932 deprived all the craftsmen of their orders. He, because no exception, also made all workers redundant.

In subsequence, her wife died of a serious illness, leaving him and four children in the big wooden factory on their own. The youngest child was 6 years old and the eldest was 15 years old. In face of misfortune, he was hesitant: if he was unable to start again, then will find a job to do.

By accident, he met his friend Dunant who worked at Industrial Association. Dunant told to him, "With such a excellent skill, you cannot give up your familiar work. It is viable to make the less costly small products that necessary for family use."

He sounded that interesting. Returning home and seeing his children playing games with toys, he suddenly realized that he should make toys the main products of his business. He thought, "Playing is the nature of children. Toys are always important friends for children who cannot live

41

玩具始终是孩子们最重要的伙伴，无论何时，孩子们都不能没有玩具。"可家人和朋友听后都反对，他们都嫌儿童玩具不赚钱，这样做只会重蹈破产的覆辙。但他坚持己见，开始将自己精细的木制手艺和艺术感全部应用在制作木制玩具上。

重新开张的木制厂成了真正的"玩具王国"，由于质优价廉，深受孩子们的喜爱，销量比以前做木制家具还大。1940 年 4 月 9 日，丹麦被德军占领，政府禁止进口外国玩具，而且还禁止在玩具中使用金属和橡胶。这无疑给他的工厂带来了好的发展机会，他的木制玩具销量两年间就翻了一倍。

然而厄运再次降临，1942 年一个风高夜黑的夜晚，不知是谁把火源带进了工厂，燃尽了所有的产品和设备，工厂一夜之间几乎化为灰烬。他站在工厂的废墟上整整一天，欲哭无泪，他决定放弃自己所追求的事业，带上几个孩子远走他乡。

就在他收拾行李准备离开的时候，一名雇员走了进来，雇员对他说道："你可以一走了之，但你这样的做法会给我们留下坏印象，那就是在困难面前的怯懦和对员工的不负责！你以前所有的努力都是白费！"他走到门口一看，留下来的十几名工人正站成一排望着他，眼里满是期待和鼓励，他决定重整旗鼓。

在家人和雇员的帮助下，他的工厂奇迹般地在废墟上重建了。生产的"悠悠"玩具曾经红极一时，但没过多久，"悠悠"风潮戛然而止。望着仓库里堆积如山的"悠悠"，他懊丧地拿过一个一劈两半，忽然发现它当作玩具卡车的轮子再合适不过了，他心想："与其重新建造木制玩具生产线，还不如放弃它们专门生产积木。"

随后工厂增加了一些现代化的大型生产设备，并开始尝试生产用塑料砖块进行拼砌的玩具，虽然规模有限，雇员不多，但是极富凝聚力

without toys anytime." But his families and friends opposed this idea, because toys were not profitable and he was likely to lead to his bankruptcy again. But he insisted on his decision and made wooden toys with all his refined skills and art.

The reopened wood factory really became a "kingdom of toys". Because of the reasonable price, his toys were widely accepted by children and the sales were even greater than that of the wooden furnitures. On April 9th, 1940, Demark was occupied by German armies and the government prohibited toys import and the use of metals and rubbers. This undoubtedly created good opportunities for the development of his factory and the sales doubled just within two years.

But misfortune cast a shadow once again. On a dark evening of 1942, somebody set fire to the factory, burning all the products and equipments and the whole factory was burnt to ashes in one night. He stood on the ruins a whole day, crying but failing to shed a tear. He wanted to give up the career he pursued and brought his children to a place far from his hometown.

When packing his luggage, one employee came in, telling to him, "You can just go away. But this will only impress us with an irresponsible coward in the face of hardship! All your efforts made would be in vain!" He stepped to the door. Saw over ten employees standing in a row looking up at him with anticipation and encouragement, he determined to get back to business with full energies.

With the help of his families and employees, his factory was miraculously rebuilt on ruins. Product "Yoyo" enjoyed popularity for a time. Sooner or later, the fancy to "Yoyo" stopped suddenly. Looking at "Yoyos" piling like a hill, he was so upset that he split them in two one by one. However, it occurred to him that "Yoyo" could be used as the wheels of toy trunks. He thought: rather than rebuild a production line of wooden toy, it would be better to give them up by focusing solely on toy building blocks.

Later, some sets of modern equipment for large-scale production were installed in the factory and he attempted to produce plastic bricks as substitutes. Although employees were restricted by production scale

和团队精神。每天早晨开始工作之前，他和所有的雇员都要聚集在一起开一个简短的祈祷会，这个习俗一直沿袭了几十年。

有一次，他的大儿子在给一个鸭子玩具喷漆时节省了一道工序，儿子高兴地告诉他为公司节省了开支。他生气地说："你为什么这么做？"儿子解释道："我只不过给鸭子涂了两次漆，而不是常规的三次。"

他立即命令道："马上去取回那些鸭子，涂上最后一遍漆，然后再重新包装好给客户送过去。所有的这些工作都必须由你自己完成，即使是通宵也要完成。"儿子听后只得乖乖地去照做了。由于他强抓管理，注重质量和诚信，所以销量和利润在玩具市场一直处于攀升状态，从小工厂到大公司，规模越来越大。

这家公司就是世界上著名的乐高玩具公司，他就是公司创始人克里斯第森。

从木制厂到大公司，从小木匠到"玩具国王"，今天的乐高在世界范围内拥有两百万会员，被美国《财富》杂志誉为"世纪玩具"。

面对厄运的频繁降临，克里斯第森也曾彷徨过，但他最终选择了直面和承担。电影《肖申克的救赎》中有一段话："每个人都是自己的上苍，如果你自己都放弃自己了，还有谁会救你？强者自救，圣者渡人。"对克里斯第森是这样，对每个人亦然。

载于《时文选粹》

智 慧 箴 言

没有人可以打败你自己，除非你自己全线崩溃然后妥协。哪怕被灾难踩在泥土里，也要奋力拼搏，开出灿烂的花朵。

regarding the member, they cohesived with a team spirit. Before starting to work in every morning, all the employees and he would meet together for a brief prayer meeting, a tradition that lasted for decades.

Once, his eldest son told to him proudly that he had saved cost for his factory by reducing a procedure when he was painting a toy duck. He was angry, asking "why would do that?" His son explained, " I just painted the duck twice, not the regular three times."

He immediately demanded, "going and retrieving all those ducks to paint it again before repacking and sending them to customers. All this have to be done on your own, even if you have to stay up to finish it." His son followed his order in accordance. Thanks to his strict management, focus by quality and integrity, his factory witnessed an upward trend in terms of sales and profit in the toy market, developing from a small factory into a large company with a growing scale.

This company is the world-renowned toy company Lego, and he is Ole Kirk Christiansen, a founder of the company.

From a wooden factory to a large company, from an unknown craftsman to the "King of Toys", now Lego has over 2 million members worldwide and is accredited as "Toy of the Century" by *Fortune* Magazine.

Facing the frequent occurrence of misfortune, Christiansen also wandered and hesitated. But finally he chose to face it and carry on. There is a statement in the movie *The Shawshank Redemption*, "Everyone is his own God. If you give up, who will save you? It takes a strong man to save himself and a great man to save others." It is the same for Christiansen and everyone else.

No one can defeat you unless you break down and compromise. Even if you are trampled in the mud, you must strive hard to make brilliant flowers.

找个合适的位置

文 / 潜川游子

> 命运不允许我们做出其他的选择，我们只能勇往直前。
>
> ——谚语

这个世界上，有一些人，他们具有贝壳一样的智慧，总能把受过的伤凝成珍珠。

1998 年，12 岁的罗伯特·帕丁森成了一名模特。当时，他的个子已经很高，并且有一张俊美得像女孩子一样的面庞。当时的英国，中性是很酷的，中性美极为流行，所以，找他签约的模特公司特别多，他迅速在英国蹿红。

几乎没费力气，他就站到了成功的巅峰，无数的鲜花与掌声，闪花了他年少纯净的眼睛。

然而，四年后，忽然所有公司都不再和他签约了。因为，整整四年过去了，他已经长成了一位帅气而阳刚的小伙子。中性美，他再也不具备了。他陷入了深深的失落之中，他实在想不通，阳刚俊美的面庞居然成了事业的绊脚石！

他彻底失业了。寂寞的时候，他就坐在屋后的小山上，蓝天白云下，

Find a Proper Place

Destiny leaves no other options for us, so we have to move on bravely.

——Proverb

There are some people in the world, who like a shell, are always wise enough to turn injuries into pearls.

In 1998, 12-year-old Robert Pattinson became a model. At that time, he was quite tall with a delicate face that liked a girl. In Britain at the time, neutral beauty was cool and quite popular. So, many model companies queued up to sign him, which making him the limelight quickly.

With few efforts to reach the peak of success, countless flowers and applauses flashed his young and pure eyes.

However, four years later, no company continued to contract with him all of a sudden because he grew up into a handsome young man. Neutral beauty was no longer his trait. Deeply lost in distress, he had no idea why such a handsome face would become the stumbling block of his career.

He was completely out of work. When he was lonely, he would sit on the hill behind the house with a sadness forming on his brow under the blue sky. His father, putting aside his business, came back to comfort him. Looking at his father who was so kind and generous, finally he cried

眉宇间是深深的忧伤。父亲放下了生意，赶回来安慰他，看着慈祥宽厚的父亲，他终于无助地落下了泪水："难道长得阳光帅气也是罪过吗？"

"不，宝贝，阳刚帅气是你的优点，这也是我和你妈妈最大的骄傲。"父亲目光沉静，语调舒缓："但是孩子你要记住，就算是优点，如果放在了不合适的地方，也会成了缺点！"

"不合适的地方？"罗伯特大睁着明亮的泪眼看着父亲。

"是的！阳刚帅气的造型放到崇尚中性美的模特界，就成了缺点。但是换个地方呢？比如说表演戏剧或电影……"

罗伯特觉得眼前一下子亮堂了，迎着春风，他微笑着擦干了泪水。

从此，罗伯特一心扑到了影视表演上，然而，这条路是坎坷的。有一次，他好不容易被一位印度女导演相中，参与了名著改编片《名利场》的拍摄。但是，罗伯特的戏少得可怜，然而就是这少得可怜的戏份最后也被剪掉了，他仅仅出现在了 DVD 版中。

但是，罗伯特一直在坚持，他就像贝壳一样，在黑暗中默默聚集着力量。

2008 年，在浪漫奇幻电影《暮光之城》中，罗伯特饰演神秘迷人又邪气俊美的吸血鬼——爱德华·卡伦，终于取得了巨大的成功。他阳刚迷人的扮相迷倒了全球亿万影迷，被美国《时代》杂志评为最性感的男明星，成为全球新一代的青春偶像，他终于为自己阳刚帅气的面庞找到了合适的位置。

人要有贝壳般的智慧，为自己找一个合适的位置，即便是伤口，也能凝作珍珠。

载于《思维与智慧》

智慧箴言

每个人都是独一无二的，那些熠熠生辉的闪光点，如果找到合适的舞台，就会最大化地成就自己。

helplessly, "Is it a fault to grow young and handsome?"

"It isn't, baby. Handsomeness and masculinity are your trait and also the biggest pride of your mother and me." With calmness in his eyes, he spoke slowly, "But you have to remember, is merits will become demerit if placed at an improper place!"

"Improper place?" Robert looked at his father with his bright eyes wide open.

"Yes! Once put in the model industry which advocates neutral beauty, a handsome and masculine face become a weakness. But how about turn to another fields, such as performance, drama or movies…"

Robert suddenly felt everything in the ahead were optimistic. He wiped away his teas the smiled against the spring breeze.

From then on, Robert focused on movies, but it was a rough and bumpy road. Once, he managed to take part in the famous adaptation film *"Vanity Fair"* at the approval of a female Indian director. However, he just acted in a few scenes. But even these few scenes were cut off, only reserved in the DVD version.

Despite so, Robert insisted on it just as a shell, consolidating power quietly in the darkness.

In 2008, he acted a mysterious, charismatic and handsome vampire Edward Cullen in the romantic fiction *"The Twilight"* and made a great success. His masculinity was appealed by tens of millions of fans globally. Renowned as the sexiest actor by *Time* Magazine, he became a youth idol of the new generation worldwide. Finally he put his handsome face to a proper place.

Man has to be as wise as a shell so as to find a proper place. Even an injury can be turned into a pearl.

Every one is unique with sparkling points. Stand on a right stage, and you can make the best of yourself.

最美丽的交际——尊人显三度

文 / 张盼

> 人应尊敬他自己，并应自视能配得上最高尚的东西。
>
> ——黑格尔

放低姿态，尊人显风度

1998 年，一个 28 岁的年轻人找了几个朋友合伙开了一家小网络公司，一次偶然的机会他去参加一个有关互联网的企业家交流会。

在交流会当天，年轻人不禁发现自己很是寒碜，其他人个个西装革履，衣着光鲜。而自己由于刚刚创业并没有多少钱，只穿着一件普通并且有点旧的黑色夹克，在会场中显得格格不入。年轻人有意坐在会场的一个角落，以避免引起更多人的注意。

交流会结束后，大家都在忙着互换名片，根本没有人注意他。他起身准备离开，突然一个声音传来："嗨，小伙子，干吗这么急着走，我还没认识你们这些青年才俊呢。"

年轻人转身望去，只见一个老人边说边笑地看着他，年轻人仔细看了看，这个老人就是刚才第一个上台发言的企业家啊。年轻人又惊又

The Most Beautiful Communication—Respect to Show Your Attitudes

People should respect himself, and be able to adapt himself to the highest quality.

——Hegel

Putting a low profile, which can show your grace

In 1998, a 28-year-old young man established a small IT company with several friends. By chance, he participated in an exchange conference for IT entrepreneurs.

On that day, he could not help feeling that he was scrubby, as others were well dressed in suits and ties. However, he could only wear normal and a bif old jacket became he had little money as a start-up. This made him out of place in the hall; therefore he sat in a corner to avoid others' attention.

After the meeting, every one was busy exchanging business cards so that nobody was aware of him. When he started to leave, a voice came, "Hey, young man! Why do you leave so anxiously? Give me a chance to know younger talents like you."

Turning around, he saw an old man looking at him with smiles. Looking at him carefully, the young man found that he was the entrepreneur who first made a speech on the stage. Surprised and delighted, he blurted out, "Nice to meet you. Anything can I do for you?"

喜，脱口而出道：

"您好，您找我有事吗？"

"没什么特别的事，主要是想和你们年轻企业家聊聊，年轻人还是有想法的。"老企业家爽朗地笑道。

年轻人只得说出实情："其实，我不是什么企业家，对互联网了解的也不深，我只是开了个小公司，来这里学习学习。"

"哦，是这样。"老企业家若有所思地点点头，马上又提高声音说道："不懂没关系，企业家有不懂的很正常，慢慢学嘛。这是我的名片，请收下。"

年轻人惊愕地看着这位老企业家，不禁被他的尊重和谦逊所感动。他回到公司后，把老企业家的名片放在自己的办公桌上，时刻提醒自己要像老人一样做个谦逊和尊重别人的人。

十几年过去了，年轻人成了互联网领军人物之一，他就是知名天使投资人，360公司董事长周鸿祎。

周鸿祎常在演讲中提起那次令他尴尬又备受鼓舞的企业家交流会，他说，一张名片有多重？拿在手中很轻很轻，但老企业家称他为企业家并给他名片时让他有了无比的自信和勇气。这一路走来，他深深感受到这张名片所承载的重量。

转换角度，尊人显大度

1993年，一个从农村走出来的小伙子怀着对表演的热爱，报考北京电影学院，初试没过，就待在北京流浪，跑龙套，当群众演员。

一次，年轻人又有机会去当群众演员了，他兴奋不已。在拍摄时，他只有三五秒的镜头，但是他依旧很用心。可令人没想到的是，在拍摄过程中，由于年轻人不小心，碰撞到了主演。导演一看，竟是个群众演员撞到了主演，顿时怒从中来，指着年轻人的鼻子骂道："你一个跑龙套的，怎么这么不长眼？"

"No, there is nothing particular. I just want to talk with young entrepreneurs like you are always thoughtful." The old businessman laughed heartily.

To be true to himself, the young man said, "Actually, I am not an entrepreneur and has no deep understanding about the Internet. I only set up a small company and come here to learn from you."

"Ok, I get it." The old businessman nodded his head as if thinking of something. Then he raised his voice, saying "It is ok to know little about it. It is usual for a businessman to get a blind point. You just learn about it. This is my name card, please take it."

Looking at this old businessman with a great surprise, the young man was touched by his respect and humility. When he returned to his company, he put the old man's name card on his desk to remind himself of being a man as humble and respectful as the old man.

Over ten years later, this young man became one of the leaders in the Internet realm. He is Zhou Hongyi, the famous angel investor and the chairman of 360 company.

He always mentioned that made him embarrassing but inspiring in that exchange conference in his speeches. He usually asks how heavy is a name card is. Put it in hand is light, but when the old businessman gave the name card to him, he felt unimaginable confidence and courage. Reaching where he is today, he deeply feels the weight carried by this card.

Thinking In Others' Shoes, Respect People can Show our Tolerance

In 1993, a young man from the countryside, with a great passion for performance, applied for Beijing Film Academy. Failed after, he stayed in Beijing to play small roles and worked as a extra.

In a one day, he was excited that he could have chance to enjoy a film as a extra. In the film, though appearing only a few seconds, he still paid more attention to it. Unexpectedly, during the filming process, the young man ran into the leading actor by accident. Seeing a figurant collided hit the key actor, the director was outrageous, scolding him and pointing at his nose, "Don't you have eyes? You are a nameless figurant!"

年轻人反应过来自己碰到了主演，吓得赶忙道歉，并极力解释自己是无意的。谁知主演却走到年轻人身边，拍拍他的肩膀说道："咱们都是演员，拍戏的时候难免会有碰撞，不必往心里去。"

一股暖流瞬间涌上年轻人的心头，这是他第一次被人尊称为演员，他深深地被感动了。

一旁的其他演员很是诧异，便问主演："他碰了您，导演替您训斥他几句也无可厚非，您可倒好，还反过来安慰他。"

"不，不！"主演反驳道："虽然他碰了我，但他是无意的，我如果动怒于他反而显得我很小气。不向无意的人动怒，这应该是对别人最起码的尊重。"

年轻人惊讶地看着主演，久久说不出话来，他暗暗下了决心，从今以后，一定要做一个真正的演员。

十年后，年轻人主演了人生的第一部电影，一举夺得东京电影节金麒麟奖，并在以后的影视道路上，获得了一个又一个了不起的荣誉。他就是郭晓东，一个从山区农村走出来的小伙子。

在做人交际方面，我们应该像主演那样，在受到别人的无意冒犯时，多站在别人的角度考虑问题，用一颗平等的心尊重别人。如此，不仅你的交际之路越走越宽，还有可能成就别人。

凉菜暖心，尊人显高度

1990年，一个年轻人高考落榜后，去了一个影视城做保安。他每天尽心尽职，兢兢业业，但不时受到公司同事的嘲笑和讥讽，年轻人却早已习惯这种生活。

一天早上，影视城经理宣布，为了激励员工的积极性，将选一部分优秀员工晚上去星级酒店和董事长共进晚餐，所有人都激动不已，希望这次机会能轮到自己。

年轻人心想，自己只是个没人注意的保安，肯定没机会去和董事

He was frightened so he began to apologize when he realized his physical collision with the leading actor and explained that he was unaware of it. Unexpectedly, the leading actor came near to him and tapped him on the shoulder, saying, "We are both actors. It is normal to have physical collisions. You don't mind it."

With the warmth inside, he was deeply moved, because this was the first time for him to be referred as an actor.

Other actors were surprised that they asked the leading actor, "he crashed you, so it is understandable that the director gives him a dressing-down. But how could you comfort him instead?"

"Well", the actor refuted, "it is unintentional for him to crash me. Getting angry out of it will only look at I'm stingy and mean. It is the basic respect not being angry for those who aer without intentions."

Surprisingly, the young man looked at the actor without saying a word for a long time. He made up his mind to become a real actor from then on.

Ten years later, he starred the first movie in this life, which won the "Tokyo Sakura Grand Prix". Following on, he was accredited with many other marvelous honors. He is Guo Xiaodong, a young man from a rural village.

We should learn from the leading actor in our interpersonal relations. When somebody offends you unconsciously, you should consider it from his/her perspective and respect him/her with equanimity. By doing that, not only will you be more communicative,but also be able to achieve others..

Cold Dishes can Warm Your Heart, Respect People can Show Our Elegance

In 1990, a young man became the security guard of a studio when he failed to be enrolled in universities. Despite working with diligence each day, he was still ridiculed by other colleagues sometimes. But he had already been accustomed to this kind of life.

In a one morning, the manager announced that in order to inspire the activity of employees, some of the excellent staffs would have the chance to have a dinner with the company's president in a star restaurant. Everyone was thrilled and hoped to get this opportunity.

长共餐。他觉得如果别人去聚餐放松，自己应该请个假休息休息，毕竟自己每天兢兢业业地工作，也很劳累。

年轻人中午来到经理办公室，说明来意，经理反问道："怎么突然要请假呢？"

年轻人反应过来，今晚有不少人去聚餐，影院人手紧缺，经理肯定不轻易准假。于是急中生智道："呃，那个，我身体有点不舒服。"

"哦，这样啊。"经理遗憾地摇摇头。

年轻人心里一惊，莫非经理已经察觉到自己在撒谎。

"身体不适的话，那就好好休息吧。"经理拍了拍年轻人的肩膀，继续说道："你今晚去不了的话，我让小陈帮你带些酒店的特色菜和好酒回来，不过，带回来时饭菜可能会凉，热一热再吃。"

年轻人顿时明白过来，当他无意中放弃与董事长进餐的机会，经理在为他惋惜的同时，还考虑到让别人帮他带些饭菜回来，而他只是一个小小的保安，这不禁使年轻人深受感动。

很多年过去了，这个年轻人一路坎坷，一路奋斗，最终成为中国著名的主持人之一，他就是孟非。

在我们平时生活中，"帮你带些饭菜回来"，这是朋友之间最熟悉不过的对话，可这句话让孟非牢记至今，因为这是一个经理对一个保安的关心与尊重。孟非后来在一次访谈节目中说，当时的他只是一个小保安，他以为没人会关心他，尊重他。可那天晚上，经理让同事带回来的饭菜虽然已经是凉的，却温暖了他的心。

载于《做人与处世》

智 慧 箴 言

> 尊重别人，显示的却是自己的修养和品格。一个尊重别人的人，精神上是有高度的。

The young man thought that he was an obscure security guard, it was impossible for him to have a dinner with the president. He felt that if someone went to a dinner party, he should ask for taking a break, after all he worked hard everyday.

Coming to the manager's office in the noon, the young man explained the reason for being here. But the manager asked, "Why do you suddenly ask for a leave?"

He thought it must be difficult for him to get the permission, since the cinema is shorthanded because so many people go dinning together tonight. With a quick wits, he responded, "I feel uncomfortable."

"Ok, I understand it." said the manager, shaking his head regrettably.

Startled, the young man thought could it be that the manager had detected his lie?

"Taking a good rest if you feel sick." tabbing him on the shoulder, the manager continued, "if you cannot come tonight, I'll ask Xiaochen to bring back for you some special dishes and good wine of the dinner. But the dishes may turn cold when brought back, so you need to heat them before eating."

He suddenly understood that he gave up the chance to dine with the president without awareness. While feeling sorry for him, the manager still considered to ask somebody else to bring back him some food. He was just a nameless security guard, he felt deeply touched by the manager's consideration.

Years later, marching on a tough road, the young man became one of the famous hosts in China with strenuous and continual efforts. His name is Meng Fei.

In daily life, "I bring you some food" could be the most usual expression between friends. But it deeply entrenched on the mind of Meng Fei till today, because it embodies the manager's care and respect to a security guard. Meng Fei once said in an interview, he was just an unknown guard at that time, he thought nobody would care or respect him. But in that evening, though the food brought back was cold, it still warmed his heart.

Respecting others shows your characters and morals. A respectful man is inspirational and motivational.

尊重有规矩的人

文 / 痴情小木子

> 矩不正，不可为方；规不正，不可为圆。
>
> ——淮南子

抗日战争爆发后，著名文史大师刘文典没来得及与清华、北大等高校师生撤离南下，滞留北平，生活窘迫的他被一家米店老板聘请当私塾先生。

米店老板虽然小气，但也算守规矩，从不克扣店员伙计的工钱，对刘文典也很尊敬。1937 年 7 月 29 日，北平沦陷后，老板为躲避战乱突然举家而逃，好端端的米店扔下了。

店员、伙计慌了神，有人提议："发财要趁早，现在老板不在，我们分了钱财作鸟兽散，那可是笔大数目，说不定就是日后的'第一桶金'。"

此时，刘文典站出来说："君子爱财，取之有道，凡事都有规矩，老板以前从没亏待过大家，我们应该尊重有规矩的人。现在我们不能因为没了老板而乱了米店的规矩，大家应该团结起来，将米店继续经营下去，待老板回来我们也好交代。"

Respect People With Rules

No rules, no standards.

——Huai Nanzi

After the outbreak of the Chinese People's War of Resistance against Japanese Aggression, the well-known literature and history master Liu Wendian, failing to retreat to southern China with teachers and students of Tsinghua and Beijing Universities and other institutes of high education, stranded in beiping. Struggling with life, he was forced to be employed as a private tutor by the owner of a rice shop.

Although the owner was quite stingy, also counts the rules, he never deducted clerk's wages, also quite respected to Liu Wendian. On July 29, 1937, after the fall of beiping,the owner fleded from the fighting and threw down the rice shop.

The clerks panicked, some of then said shat "We should take time to make profits. Since the owner has left, we should split the large sum of money. which can be used as 'the first bucket of gold'."

At this moment, Liu Wendian stepped forward, saying, "A gentleman makes money through honorable means. Everything has its rules. The owner treated us well, so we should respect people with rules. Now, we cannot break the shop's rules in his absence. Instead, it is advisable for us to join hands together to continue the business of the rice shop so that we can live up to the owner's expectation when he returns."

众人觉得刘文典说得有理，于是包括刘文典在内的几个人将米店局面给撑起来了，使得米店照常运转。半年后，躲过风声的老板终于露了面，此时，米店依然照常运转，钱、物、账都清清楚楚地完璧归赵。

　　刘文典此时刚好接到西南联大的通知，要他南下归校，他听到这个消息很高兴，但又有点沮丧，因为他此刻身无分文，没有上路的盘缠。老板听说后拿出一笔钱给刘文典，老板说："我不在的时候，多亏了你，不然这米店的规矩就坏了。我尊重有规矩的人，这些钱你就拿去当盘缠吧。"

　　米店老板遵守规矩，不克扣员工的工资，从而赢得了大家的尊重，使得米店照常运转；刘文典遵守规矩，劝说大家一起守规矩，继续经营米店，从而赢得了老板的尊重。生活中，你若能遵守规矩，就会赢得别人的信赖，人们都尊重有规矩的人。别人才会放心地将事情托付给这样的人。

载于《思维与智慧》

智慧箴言

　　不守规矩不成方圆，遵守规矩就是信守承诺。一个信守承诺的人，是有魅力的人。

All the people agreed with him. As a result, the clerks together with Liu Wendian, supported the shop to sustain its business. Half a year later, when the owner returned back, he got the clearly recorded accounts and money earned from the normally operated rice shop and properties were still the way they used to be.

At this time, Liu Wendian was informed to return to the university of the south. He was excited but a bit of depressed that he had no money for this travel. When the owner heard about it, he gave some money to Liu Wendian, telling him, "When I left, It thanked to you that helped to uphold the rules of the shop. I respect people count the rules. So you take the money."

The owner abided by the rules and deducted the clerk's wages so that he earned the respect from people who helped sustained normal operation of the shop, Liu Wendian upheld the rules by persuading others into abiding by the rules to continue the shop's business so that he won respect from the owner. In life, if one can count rules, he will be win others' trust, and people will respect those who have rules.Others will be relieved to entrust things to that people.

No rules, no standards. Adherence to rules is to keep promises. A man keeps his words is a charming person.

亲情比成功更重要

文 / 文小圣

亲情是甜美的乳汁，抚育我们成长。

——高尔基

那年，著名导演李安构思要拍一部叫《卧虎藏龙》的影片，他首先想到的男主角人选是"功夫皇帝"李连杰。于是，他找到李连杰，跟李连杰详谈了自己影片的构想。听完李安的介绍后，李连杰对这部影片也充满了兴趣，答应出演男主角。

李安从一开始，就打算要将《卧虎藏龙》拍出最好的水平，打造精品中的精品，以冲刺奥斯卡大奖。因此，剧本一改再改，一直推迟了两年，才打算正式开拍。

充分做好所有的准备工作后，李安高兴万分地打电话给李连杰："我要告诉你一个好消息，我们已经全部准备好了，《卧虎藏龙》马上就可以开拍。相信我，这部影片会在全世界走红，会是影坛中的顶尖之作！"

然而，令李安意外的是，李连杰的答复却是："真是抱歉，我的太太怀孕了，我答应过她，如果她怀孕生小孩的话，我会推掉一年之内的所有工作，专心照顾她。所以，看来我是无缘这部构思精妙的影片了。"

Family is More Important Than Success

Family is sweet milk, tending us to grow.

———Gorky

When a famous director Ang Lee was thinking about making a film called *Crouching Tiger, Hidden Dragon,* in that year. And then, the leading actor came into his mind was Jet Li, the Kongfu Emperor. Therefore, he found Jet Li and talked with him about the idea of his him. After listening to lee's introduction, Jet Li was also full of interest in the film, and he promised to play the leadingrole.

From the word go Ang Lee was determined to achieve the best effect of the movie so as to make it had the best quality to win a Oscar. To this end, the script was revised again and again and the film started shooting until two years later.

After all the preparations work made, Ang Lee called Jet Li excitedly, "I have a piece of good news for you. We are ready to start shooting *Crouching Tiger, Hidden Dragon.* Believing in me, this movie will become a blockbuster worldwide and stand on the peak of the world of films."

However, to his great surprise, Jet responded, "I am so sorry because my wife is pregnant. I promised her that I would decline all the offers to take care of her if she was willing to give birth to a child. So, it looks like I'm out of this fancy movie."

李安愣住了，但仍然不甘心地说："可这部影片是为你量身定做的，如果你不出演，将是多么可惜！我现在全力打造这部影片，我相信只要你出演，一定会使你更具知名度，甚至好莱坞都会对你青睐有加。"

李连杰平静地说："可是我认为，没有任何成功能够比亲情更重要。"

后来，《卧虎藏龙》的男主角不得不换成了周润发。这部影片播出后，立刻引起了巨大轰动，并获得了四项奥斯卡大奖，成为奥斯卡颁奖大会上最灿烂的一道风景。

有人对李连杰说："如果当时你出演《卧虎藏龙》，在奥斯颁奖大会上最风光的人也许就是你了，但你却错过了，对此，你觉得遗憾吗？"

李连杰摇了摇头，说："不会，一个人对生命有了解的话，就不会有这样的想法。虽然错过了一个很好的机会，但我体会到了亲情的幸福，这才是最珍贵的。相反，如果当时我不是陪在太太身边好好照顾她，而是去追逐自己的名利，这才会让我一辈子都感到遗憾和愧疚。"

重视亲情，不要自私，勇于付出，你也会拥有幸福的人生。没有任何成功比亲情更重要，事业失败了可以重新再来，可一旦亲情丢失了，生活将变得冰冷，任何成功都不再有意义。因此无论什么时候，我们都要把亲情放在事业之前，因为亲情的关爱最值得珍惜。

载于《思维与智慧》

智慧箴言

我们所做的一切不过就是为了让爱自己的亲人过得更好些，没有亲人我们努力给谁看呢？

Startled, Ang Lee continued, "This movie is customized for you. How pity it is if you couldn't participate in it! I am trying my utmost for it. I truly believe that your involvement will make you a great fame and even the Hollywood would belong to you."

Jet Lee said calmly, "But in my eyes, no a success is more important than my family."

Later on, the leading role of the movie *Crouching Tiger, Hidden Dragon* was changed to Zhou Runfa. It created great sensation once it was released and won four Oscars, becoming the most splendid scenery of the Oscars.

Someone asked Jet, "if you starred in the movie, the most striking man in the Oscars Award Ceremony would be you. But you missed it, have you ever regretted about that?"

Shaking his head, Jet answered, "of course it is not. One may not think as you if he understands life. Though I missed a good chance, I experienced the happiness of being together with family, which is the most precious thing. By contrast, if I was not by her side to took a good care of my wife but to pursue fame and wealth instead, I would be regretful and ashamed throughout my life."

Cherishing your family and be selfless, and never be afriaid of contribution, you will have a happy life. No a success is more important than family. Your business can restart if it is failed, but without family, life will become cold and success will no longer meaningful. Therefore, whenever it is, we have to place family ahead of business, because family is the most precious.

what we do is just to make it better for our families. Who do we try to show to?

65

耸立于自家冰箱上的哈佛

文 / 段奇清

> 做了好事受到指责而仍坚持下去，这才是奋斗者
> 的本色。
>
> ——巴尔扎克

5 岁那年，由于张媛琦爱看动画片《葫芦娃》，爸爸就笑着对女儿说："妈妈是哈美的，媛琦是哈葫的。"因为妈妈爱看美国电视剧。小媛琦想了想："那奶奶就是'哈佛'的。"她看到奶奶常常拜佛。见女儿说得有趣，爸爸哈哈地笑了，说："我女儿真聪明，将来一定能上哈佛。"就这样，她知道了世界有一所非常好的高等学府——哈佛大学。

于是，小媛琦以她稚嫩的手，在一张纸上写下了"我要上哈佛"，然后贴在了家中的冰箱上。从此，这 5 个字就如同《西游记》中如来佛祖的 5 个手指化成的"五指山"，耸立在她家的冰箱上。不，那是一条条自信、勤奋的路，牵引着她不断向着梦想的高峰攀登。

张媛琦 1995 年出生于河北衡水，上了小学，她就像小大人一样，放学后，不是做作业就是看课外读物。每每有孩子在院子里跳绳、踢球……爸爸就会说，"媛琦，你就不和他们玩上一会儿吗？"她去了，但

Harvard standing on Refrigerator

The nature of a fighter is to persist in doing a good thing even if he is reproached for it.

——Balzac

At the age of 5, Zhang Yuanqi was fond of cartoon *Calabash Brothers*. One day, his father told to her daughter smiling, "Your mother is a pro-American culture, because she loves American drama while you are a pro-cartoon." Little Yuanqi thought, then grandma is a "pro-Buddhism", since she always saw her worship Budda. Sounding interesting, her father was laughing, "How clever is my daughter! You will go to Harvard in a one day." In this way, she learnt about there is an excellent university in the world—it is Harvard.

Therefore, Yuanqi wrote "I will go to Harvard" on a piece of paper with her young hand and then sticked it to the refrigerator. Afterwards, these five words stood on the refrigerator, just as the "Five Finger Mountain" transformed from five fingers in *Journey to the West*. But in fact, this is a journey of confidence and diligence, which guided her to realize her dreams.

Born in 1995 in Hengshui, Hebei Province, Zhang Yuanqi, just looked like a little big woman, preferred to either do homework or read extracurricular materials after school. Every time when there are children skipping rope or playing football, her father would say, "Yuanqi, why do you not play with them for a while?" She would return

不多大一会工夫又回来了。爸爸说："怎么不多玩会儿?"她看着冰箱上的那5个字,向爸爸努努嘴,爸爸在心中暗暗夸奖,女儿真懂事!

张媛琦不贪玩,可有一次她却"玩"得好远好远——"玩"到了美国。由于各项成绩优异,2009年新东方组织一次国际游学,张媛琦荣幸地成为其中一员。第一次踏上大洋彼岸的这个国家,先进的教育理念及颇吸引人的人文元素让张媛琦大开眼界,更是坚定了她圆梦哈佛的决心。

上高中二年级时,张媛琦萌生了去美国学习的想法。在她看来,去了美国也就向圆梦哈佛靠近了一步;再就是,由于和同龄的孩子们接触不多,使得她的性格偏于内向,只有到了一个全新的环境,才有机会重新展示一个全新的自己,让自己变得外向,交更多的朋友。

十四五岁的小女孩就远渡重洋,这得需要多么大的勇气,在爸爸的支持下,她终于来到了美国。

美国的高中的确能让人变得外向和充满自信。其课程都有不同的计分方式,课堂小测验、讨论都会计入总成绩。一开始,她因为害怕出错很少发言,但后来发现不说话参与分数少了,平均成绩点数就降下来了。于是她开始硬着头皮主动发言,这样一来,不仅分数上去了,更是锻炼了口才,她这才发现原来自己还挺能讲的。就这样,她从害怕课堂讨论变为盼望上讨论课。

在国内读书时每天要上什么课都有固定的课表,但在美国每个人的课表都不同,必须自己提前做好安排。有时候参加话剧、音乐剧的排练,结束时已经是晚上9点多了,她就在话剧排练间隙或在校车上写作业。在美国寄宿家庭生活中,由于她放开自己,善良热情,得到了美国叔叔阿姨等一家人非常贴心的照顾,也让她很快融入了美国的生活。

quickly after she joined them. His father said, "Just enjoy your time?" Looking at the five words on the refrigerator, she pursed her lips. Her father was very thoughtful in his heart.

Zhang Yuanqi is not playful. But a once, she took a really long journey as far as the United States. Because of her excellent performance, she had the honor to be one of the international study tour organized by New Orienta in 2009. The first moment when she stepped on the country across the Pacific Ocean, her mind was extensively broadened by advanced educational concepts and attractive cultural elements, which made her determined to study in Harvard.

In Grade 11, she came up with an idea to study in the US. From her perspective, going to the US is a step closer to Harvard. In addition, she was quite introvert resulted from the lack of contacting with children at similar ages, and only by going to a completely new environment will enable her to re-exhibit herself and become outgoing by making more friends. How brave she was for a little girl of at 14 or 15 to travel far away. With her father's support, she came to America eventually.

Indeed, an American high school can make people outgoing and full of confidence. Different courses have diverse ways of scoring and in-class tests and seminars will also be counted as a part of the final score. At first, she was so afraid of making mistakes that she seldom proposed her ideas. However, it turned out that less of class contribution would reduce the score of participation, thus dragging behind the average GPA. In light of this, she tried to speak voluntarily, which not only improved her score but also practiced her spoke English and it occurred to her that she was quite eloquent. In this way, she was gone from being afraid of class discussion to looking forward to class discussions.

Domestic schools have pre-arranged classes for each course while students in America have various schedules so that they have to make proper arrangement in advance. Sometimes, it could be 9 pm when she returned home from rehearsals of plays or music dramas. In light of this, she took time to finish her homework during the break of rehearsals or on the school bus. As a kind, open-minded girl, she was warmly received by the family of her homestay, which encouraged her integration in America quickly.

"勇于尝试新事物"，更是她高中时一面高举的旗帜。为增强人文素养，提高交际能力，张嫒琦到二手店做义工、为非洲的穷人做食品和被子；她还参加学校的打扫卫生小组，虽说累但有报酬，既锻炼了自己，也可为家庭减轻经济负担。同时，她还加入了学校的田径队、网球队；为培养自己的组织能力，她带头在学校组建了一个数学俱乐部，召集所有和她一样热爱数学的同学一起参加数学竞赛。

由此她的成绩也就更优秀，历次考试全 A 通过，GPA4.11，ACT33分（American College Test，美国高考，满分36分）。她还获得第六届丘成桐中学数学奖金奖，2014 年亚利桑那州科学人文研讨会第一名，科学奥林匹克锦标赛第三名，连续两年亚利桑那州数学竞赛 25 强得主……

更令人钦佩的是，张嫒琦已被哈佛大学、麻省理工学院、斯坦福大学、康奈尔大学、卡内基梅隆大学等 9 所大学录取。2014 年全国 939万学子走进高考考场时，她这个身高 1.72 米、"美范儿"十足的美国圣格雷戈里大学预备高中学生已经在筹备去哈佛的旅程了。

张嫒琦说，5 岁时贴着的"我要上哈佛"的纸条至今还在家中的冰箱上。人们说：张嫒琦的哈佛就耸立在她家的冰箱上。

一个敢于有梦，不惧追梦的人，就一定有圆梦的那一天。

载于《文苑》

智慧箴言

　　每个人都有梦想，或者是成为什么样的人，或者是去什么不知名的远方。怕什么呢，努力就好了，今天不行，明天不行，那就积蓄力量，等到明年后年，总有一天会实现梦想。

"Bold enough to try new things" is her a high flag in high school. In order to strengthen her humanity attainment and social skill, she served as a volunteer in thrift shop and made food and quilts for the poor in Africa. Meanwhile, she also took part in school cleaning team. Although fatigued, she could get paid to reduce the financial pressure of her family while practicing herself. She also participated in the athletic team, and tennis team. For the purpose of cultivating her organization ability, she initiated a mathematic club in school to summon all those students who passionate about math to engage in math competitions.

All these made her study at ease with enhanced performance. She got A for all the exams with GPA of 4.11 and ACT of 33 (the US university entrance exam with a total score of 36). She was also awarded with the golden medal for mathematics of the 6th Shing-Tung Yau Middle School, the first prize in 2014 science and humanity seminar of Arizona, the 3rd prize in science Olympic championship and one of the top 25 performers in mathematic competition of Arizona successive 2 years…

It was impressive that Zhang Yuanqi was admitted by 9 universities, including Harvard, MIT, Stanford, Cornell, and Carnegie Mellon. When 9.39 million students entered the college entrance examination hall in 2014, her 1.72-meter-tall, American prep high school student at St. Gregory University in the United States was already preparing for a trip to Harvard.

Zhang Yuanqi said, the note " I will go to Harvard" she wrote when she was 5 was still on the refrigerator in her home. People say that her Harvard is standing on the refrigerator.

One bold enough to have and pursue a dream will eventually realize it one day.

Everyone has a dream, or dream to become somebody or go somewhere afar. Just make efforts, and there is nothing to be afraid of. If it cannot come true today or tomorrow, accumulate your efforts until next year or the year after next, it will eventually be fulfilled.

第二辑 锁不住的财富之门

Series 2　Unchained Door of Wealth

　　在这个流光溢彩的城市中，他无疑是挣扎在社会底层的小人物，重度的身体残障更是给他的生活刻上了卑微的烙印。但是，他的梦想却从来都不曾卑微。或许，他的梦想只能停留在幻想的美好世界中，但那又有什么关系？因为正是那些可能一生也实现不了的梦想，才让他有了拼搏的力量，带着回报母爱的心愿，一步一步艰难却执着地行走在人生的道路上。

　　In the splendid city, he is undoubtedly a small potato struggling at the bottom of the society severe disability further engrave his life with a humble imprint. But his dreams are never inferior. Maybe his dream can only stay in a wonderful world of fantasy, but what does it matter? Because of those dreams that may not be realized all his life, he has the strength to fight. With the desire to return the mother's love, step by step, but persistently walk on the road of life.

退步原来是向前

文 / 李红都

业精于勤，荒于嬉。

> ——韩愈

技校毕业那年，他刚满 19 岁，分到一家大型国企的分厂磨加工工序生产滚子产品。车间多是国产的老式磨床，操作技术也很简单，实习时他就开过类似的机床，所以来这里没多久，他便能独当一面，开始独立赚工时。

车间里有几位和他差不多大的年轻职工，干着和他一样简单的滚子加工工序，每天上班干活，下班走人，业余就凑在一起打扑克、下棋消磨时光。周日，小伙子们陪着各自的女朋友看电影、逛街……没有生存的压力，也没有什么惊喜，日子过得波澜不惊。轻闲之余，他有些失落——难道一辈子就这样平凡得近乎平庸地度过吗？

单位引进了几台数控车床，想进步的他主动要求调过去学习新技能。"知情"者劝他：这是个刚组建的新车间，人员少，工作量大，更重要的是，之前已掌握的磨加工技术到了这儿可就派不上用场了，得重新学习数控技术，那可不是好学的。他笑了笑，没说话。

Setback is Actually Progress

Business is idle in hours.

——Han Yu

He was just 19 when he graduated from a technical school and was assigned to a large state-owned company for grinding and processing to produce roller products. The factory was equipped mainly with easily operated old grinding machines. He had operated these kinds of grinding machines when he worked as an intern. Therefore, not long after he came here, he was able to work independently.

There were several young employees at similar ages as him, who undertook the same simple processing work of roller processing process. They came to work and left for home on time and played pokers or chess to kill the time. On Sunday, these young men would go to a movie or go shopping with their girlfriends. Without living pressure or surprises, they led a simple life. When he was free, he was quite upset—It is possible to spend his life in such an ordinary and almost mediocre way?

When some numerical controlled lathes were introduced, he volunteered to be transferred to learn about the new skills. Some informed workers persuaded him: It is a newly built factory with limited employees and large working load. More importantly, the already acquired grinding skills are not applicable to the new machines. You have to learn about the numerical technology and it is not easy to learn. He smiled without responses.

调到新车间后，他才发现有主动学习新技能的员工可真不多——整个分厂数百名员工，报名来新车间的带上他一共才四人！走近刚开封的数控车床旁，看着车间领导充满期待的目光和计划员手里那张刚签下的精车套圈产品订单，他能感到肩上那份沉甸甸的压力。

那是一段充满激情的时光，白天他跟着厂家人员学习实践操作，不懂的地方就记在小本子上，晚上上网搜索答案，还找来数控机床理论知识书籍查寻答案，直到把当天没弄明白的地方全搞清楚才肯休息。第二天一大早，又匆匆赶到单位，投入实操培训当中。培训结束后，他们四人开始试车生产加工新订单。因为工作和学习忙，周日也没空陪女朋友，惹得女孩儿委屈得直哭，他安慰她，他这么努力，才是对另一半负责任……

为了保证及时交货，加班加点是家常便饭。往往其他车间周日都休息了，他们车间仍是机床轰鸣。最初的两个月，尽管他们四人都非常勤奋，但因为技术不熟练，生产效率并不高，勉强能完成工时定额。

看到他没有节假日，没有礼拜天，每天泡在数控车间忙得焦头烂额，工资却并不比之前干滚子磨加工工序时拿的多，有人就笑他，放着轻松简单的活儿不干，非得去新车间干那又重又累的活儿。重新学一门设备的操作知识，工资还没以前高，这样的生活状态不是退步是什么？真是冒傻气！

面对讥笑，他选择了沉默，用布袋和尚的诗激励自己——"手把青秧插满田，低头便见水中天；心地清净方为道，退步原来是向前。"

三个月后，他终于摸透了数控车床的脾性，半年后，他的工时开始从车间脱颖而出。因为他平时善于理论联系实际，遇到什么操作上的难题，都喜欢在网上或翻书寻求理论的支撑，所以他的数控理论知识体系很全面。每逢分厂有加工难度大的产品，车间主任第一个想到的就是他。

When he was transferred, he found only a small number of employees willing to learn new skills—only four people signed up, he including him, among hundreds of new workers. He approached the newly opened unmerical control lathe room looking at the shop leader's expectant gaze and the order for the product of the finished car ring that had just been signed by the planner. He could feel the heavy burden on his shoulders.

The days were filled with passion when he learnt about machine operation from factory personnel and made a note of what he failed to understand in a small notebook during the day. In the evening, he searched answers online or find books on theoretical knowledge of the CNC machine tool and would not sleep until he understood all the question in the day. Early in the tomorrow morning the other day, he would rush to the factory for practice training. The four people began to make products for the new order after training. Preoccupied with work and study, he had no time to accompany his girlfriend even on Sunday. The girlfriend grieved and wept. He comforted her that he worked so hard to be responsible for her...

To ensure delivery upon time, it was usual to work overtime. When other workshops were empty on Sunday, their workshop was still filled with the roaring of lathes. In the first two months, although all four of them were very diligent, the working time quota can be barely complete because the technology is not skilled, the production efficiency is not high. Without holidays or weekends, and with a salary lower than the time when he worked in grinding process, he was ridiculed by others that it was such a fool like him and a setback in his life as he, giving up the easy tasks, chose to assume the heavy and tiresome work in the new workshop and learnt the operation of a new machine, which earned him less. Learn a new knowledge of the operation of a device, the salary is not as high as before. It's such a state of life a step backwards? That's stupid.

Being derided, he chose to say nothing but motivated himself with the poet wrote by Budai—"planting the green seedlings in fields with hands, one can see the sky in water when bows his head. With a clear mind inside, one will find a step backward is actually progress forward."

Three months later, he finally mastered how to control and operate the digital controlled lathe. Half a year later, his work efficiency stood out from the workshop. As he was prone to linking theories to practice and

一年后，公司组织各分厂的数控车间操作工参加公司级数控技术比赛，凭着出色的操作经验和丰富的理论知识，他一举夺魁，登上全公司数控技术比赛冠军的宝座。当年，年仅21岁的他因出色的技术和工作表现被推选为首席员工，成了全公司最年轻、最有前途的金领技工。

没多久，公司开始在全厂范围推广数控技术，老机床大面积停产，之前不愿学新知识的工友随时面临被行业淘汰出局的危机，那些曾笑他"退步"的工友，此时此刻才明白——真正退步的不是一时工资落后的他，而是像自己这样死抱着一门老技术，不肯更新知识的人。

如今，他一个人熟练而轻松地掌控着两台数控机床，拿着常人两倍的工资，令工友们羡慕之余，心生敬意，也令女朋友眼含崇拜，满心欢喜……

不错，人生像极了农夫插秧，当我们身心不为外界物欲所左右，能够无视闲言碎语，心无旁骛地一根接一根往下插时，就是生存和发展之道相契的时候。表面上看，我们像农夫一样边插边后退，可也正是因为这样一门心思地退后才能把稻秧全部插好，所以才有了真正意义上的前进！智慧的职场生涯也是这样，不是只一味地向前冲，有的时候，若能退一步思考问题，往往会拥有更为海阔天空的新天地。

载于《文苑》

智慧箴言

人生需要退步，当在某一项事业上再没上升空间的时候，我们就得考虑去重新开始另一项技能。就像装满水的杯子，只有倒掉，才可以装进去新鲜的水。退步，是不满足现状，积极进取的表现。

finding theoretical support both online and from books whenever he met a problem, he had a comprehensive sytem of digital control theoretical knowledge. Every time when there were products difficult to produce, he was the first man came into the mind of the director. One year later, the company organized operators from different workshops to participate in the competition of numerical control lathe operation and won the first prize. In that year, with excellent skills and performance, he was elected the chief employee at the age of 21, becoming the youngest and the most promising technician with a competitive salary.

Soon the company began to introduce numerical control technology on a large scale. As a result, conventional lathes were no longer used and workers who refused to learn new skills were facing the threat of redundancy. Those who used to ridicule him as making a step backward how realized—the one who step backward was not him whose salary was reduced for a short time, but the one who refused to learn new skills, depending solely on an old technique.

Today, he controls two numerical control machine skillfully and easily with doubled salary when compared to ordinary workers. This makes other workers enviable and respectful and her girlfriend is now adored him with happiness…

Undoubtedly, life is like a farmer just planting seedlings. When we ignore the external material world and gossip to focus on planting, we can strike a balance between existence and development. Superficially, we, just like farmers, can plant while stepping back. But this enables us to concentrate on planning when stepping backward, which actually creates steps forward! It is the same for the wisdom in career path. Instead of rushing forward, sometimes one step backward can broaden a new world for you.

Life needs a step back. When there is no room for growth in a cause, we have to consider starting another skill. It is just like a cup filled with water, only when the water is poured out, the fresh water can be put in it. A step back is a performance that is not satisfied with the status quo.

做好分内事就能感动世界

文 / 梅若雪

做好每一件该做的事就是责任。

——王爱珍

1998 年，韩三平、张艺谋带了一个由三十多人的中国电影代表团访问美国。

在进行电影艺术交流时，听说王洛勇正在百老汇主演音乐剧《西贡小姐》。这可是一个不容错过的机会，他们很想欣赏王洛勇的演出。

然而，接待单位难以办到：百老汇的戏票价高达 120 美元，30 多个人对方还真请不起，而且王洛勇的戏，票是限购的。"那么直接找王洛勇吧！"有人提议说。

王洛勇待人一向热情豪爽，况且是国内来的人，他立刻满口应承下来，并表示这是应该尽的地主之谊。王洛勇立即去办，到百老汇剧院票房去预订当天晚上的票。没想到，票房的人也面有难色，说："30 多张，太多了，按我的权限一个人最多只能买到 10 张。不过，实在需要的话，请打电话到伦敦，向老板喀麦隆请示。"

接到王洛勇的电话后，喀麦隆欣然应允。拿到票后，票房的人说：

Doing a Good Job can Move the World

Responsibility is to do everything you have to do.

——Wang Aizhen

In 1998, a Chinese film delegation with more than 30 people guided by Han Sanping and Zhang Yimou visited the United States.

When making exchanges about film art, they heard that Wang Luoyong was starring in the musical "*Miss Saigon*" in the Broadway, which was an opportunity not to be missed, because they would like to see Wang's performance.

But the reception department could not make it true, since that one ticket of musicals in Broadway was so expensive and up to 120 dollars, let alone 30 people, they could not afford it. Besides, someone proposed to go straight to Wang Luoyong.

Wang Luoyong always treated people in an enthusiastic and generous manner. They were from his own country, so he promise immediately, and said he should be the host. Wang Luoyong went to the box office of the Broadway Theater immediately, booking tickets on that evening. Unexpectedly, the staff members of the box office said: "Based on my limits of authority, I can only buy 10 tickets per person. However, if necessary, you can call Cameroon in London for application."

After receiving Wang's call, Cameroon agreed joyfully. Getting the

"洛勇，这个钱你可是要自己付的，所以得从你工资里边扣除。"王洛勇笑了笑："这个当然，我可没想蹭票。"

一个星期过去了，他领到工资，回家一数，一分钱没少。他想可能是剧团忘记扣了。第二个星期，还是没少一分，这让他不安起来：别是票房把这事给疏忽了！

他连忙去问，对方告诉他："没错的，那钱喀麦隆先生为你垫付了。"他一下子愣在那里，有一种说不出的感动。

王洛勇当即把电话打给了喀麦隆先生，问他这么做的原因，喀麦隆说："因为这个戏你演了三年却没有请过一天病假，我感谢你！你担任这一角色以后，所有的亚洲观众来看这个戏的，没有一个退票的，我这是感谢你啊！"听了喀麦隆的话，王洛勇感动得流泪了。

其实，人们都被王洛勇感动了，他在百老汇演《西贡小姐》，演了5年半的时间，成功演出了2478场，票房收入达3.7亿美元。因此，他被美国媒体称为百老汇的"百年奇迹"。

专心致志做好分内的事，也许就能创造奇迹。

载于《当代青年》

智慧箴言

做好自己分内的事，就是为集体做了最大的贡献，自然会赢得别人的尊敬。好高骛远的人，到头来什么都干不好。

tickets, the worker said: "Luoyong, the costs of the tickets will be deducted from your salary." Wang Luoyong smiled, "Sure, I have never thought I can get them for free."

One week later, he got his salary without any deduction. He thought that the troupe might forget to deduct. While another week later, it was the same, which made him uneasy and doubted that the box office had neglected the matter.

So he asked immediately. The worker told him that Mr. Cameroon paid for him. He stood surprised a moment with an inexpressible move.

Wang Luoyong called Mr. Cameroon instantly and asked for reason. Mr. Cameroon replied, "Because you have acted in this musical for three years without one day off, I should show my gratitude. After you took this role, none of the Asian audiences who bought the tickets watched your performance have any refund, which moved me deeply. So I could express my sincere thanks to you in this way." At that moment, he was moved to tears.

Actually, audiences were all moved by Wang Luoyong. Since that he has been acted as the major role in *"Miss Saigon"* for five and half years with 2,478 sessions valued 370 million dollars, he was awarded as "a miracle in one hundred years" in Broadway by the US media.

If you concentrate on what you do, you may be able to do miracles.

Do your part,is to do the best for the team,will win the respect of others. An ambitious man can't do anything well in the end.

成长记忆里的阅读印痕

文 / 袁恒雷

> 知古不知今，谓之落沉。知今不知古，谓之盲瞽。
>
> ——王充

年少的时候，我们大多数人都会与书本画册打交道，那时的我们天真好奇，对周遭的一切都想去探知。而随着年龄的渐长，我们接触的东西会越来越多，兴趣爱好也随之有所变化，许多人对年少时的阅读兴趣愈发增强，而另一些人却喜欢上了其他的爱好。

不过我想说的是，年少时的阅读印记对所有人的影响都将是一生的，而如果我们能够把阅读的兴趣保持下来，那我们得到的裨益肯定会绵延持久，并且对我们的提升也是全方位的。

如今我刚过而立之年，所从事的职业与阅读可以说是紧密相关，身为杂志编辑，每天看文章、改文章就是我的工作。回首自己的阅读经历，我感觉的确是别有趣味，那些成长记忆里的阅读印痕在我现在的读书写作过程中时常闪现，并影响着我，也许这就是个人的阅读积淀吧。

我最开始的阅读记忆是在小学时代，作为学生，我们最基本的阅

Reading prints in the memory of growing up

Knowing that the ancients don't know today, it's sink. knowing today but don't know ancients, it's blind.

——Wang Chong

When we were young, most of us would deal with books and pictures. At that time, we were innocent and curious, and wanted to know everything around us. As we grow older, we will touch more and more things and interests will change, many people increasingly to enhance youth reading interest, while others love the other hobbies.

But I want to say is that the influence of childhood reading mark for everyone's will be a lifetime, but if we are able to keep down the interest in reading, then the benefits that we receive will certainly last for a long time, and will also enhance us in an all-round way.

Now I am just over thirty, occupation and reading can be said to be closely related, as a magazine editor, it's my job to read and change articles every day. Looking back on my reading experience, I feel really interested, the reading marks in those growing memories often flashed in my current reading and writing process, and affected me, maybe this is a personal reading accumulation.

读素材自然是各类教材，比如语文、历史、地理、自然等等。这些教材里的课文恰如我们餐桌上的主食，是我们精神食粮中最基本的，它们奠定了我对这个世界的认知。历史文化、名人轶事、天文地理、古今风物，虽然都可以说是常识性的内容，但对于孩童时期的我们来讲是极具启蒙意义的。

我就读的小学里有个图书室，我和小伙伴们在里面借阅了关于恐龙、关于中外短小故事的图书，从那里我们知晓了恐龙原来是地球被彗星撞击引发海啸洪水所灭绝的，也知道了霸王龙、雷龙、翼龙等恐龙的类别，而中外故事妙趣横生，可以说这些课外书是各种滋味迭出的佳肴。虽然我们小学图书馆里的图书有限，父母也很少给我买课外书，但这些书籍对于一个少年来讲也是足够的了，令我获益良多。

进入初高中时代后，我的阅读视野就仅限于教材书本了，因为升学压力非常大，师长们为了我们考出高分进入好学校，可以说是严格控制我们的课外书阅读。所以此时的阅读比起小学时代相对苍白了许多，但即便这样，仍然是有些素材可读的。

比如语文教材会配有选读课本，里面收录的文章比起教材更为灵动丰富，这类书籍就是为了扩大学生们阅读量的。历史、地理、物理、化学、生物等教材，每篇课文的注释、背景材料都是既有助于了解教材正文，又极具有百科性质的知识材料，这些就大大增强了教材的趣味性，也同时开阔了我们的视野。而我认为这些边边角角的材料则更为生动有趣，虽然它们在考试时很少用得上，但真的不失为一篇篇妙趣横生的知识卡片，丰富了我们的阅读世界，让仅有的阅读素材也变得张力十足。

考入大学后，面对一整座图书馆，我们就进入知识的海洋啦！而说起我本科时代的阅读体会，现在想来可远远做不到书虫的标准，并且

My earliest reading memory was in primary school. As a student, our basic reading materials are various kinds of teaching materials, such as Chinese, history, geography, nature, and so on. The texts in these textbooks are like the staple food on our table. They are the most basic part of our spiritual food. They have laid a foundation for my understanding of the world. History, anecdotes, astronomy and geography, ancient and modern scenery, although can be said to be the common content, it is very enlightening significance for us in childhood.

There is a library in my primary school, my friends and I borrowed books and short story about Chinese and foreign from which we know that the dinosaurs died out of tsumami flood caused by the comet's impact on the earth also know is the original earth by comets like Rex, Brontosaurus, wing dragon other dinosaur category, and Chinese and foreign the story can be said that these books full of wit and humour, are a delicacy of various tastes. Although our primary school library books are limited, parents seldom buy me books, but these books for a teenager are also enough, so I gained.

At the beginning of high school, my reading field of view should be confidned to the textbooks books, because of the pressures are very large to get us into a good college, teachers can be said to be strictly control the extracurricular books we read. So reading at this time is relatively pale than it was in primary school, but even so, there are still some readable material.

For example, Chinese textbooks will be provided with selected readings, and the articles included are more intelligent than those of textbooks. This kind of books is intended to expand the reading quantity for students. History, geography, physics, chemistry, biology textbooks, notes and background materials of each text are not only help to understand the text, and also has the properties of encyclopedic knowledge materials, these will greatly enhance the interest of teaching materials, and also broaden our view. And I think these corners of the material is more vivid and interesting, though they rarely use it in the exam, it is a full of wit and humour knowledge card, enrich our world of reading, so that only reading material has become full of tension.

很有趣味的是，我喜欢上了武侠书。我首选读的是金庸的书，因为金庸在许多国人的概念里，他的书籍与影视剧是武侠第一人。"飞雪连天射白鹿，笑书神侠倚碧鸳"就是我阅读金庸作品的顺序，并且大部分都看完了。

我的体会是，金庸先生之所以会受到知识界、阅读界、平民界等社会各界的好评，实在是因为其书中绝对不是简简单单的打打杀杀，而是包罗万象，极富正能量，积极宣扬中国传统文化中的"仁、义、礼、智、信、忠肝义胆、侠之大者"，批判背信弃义等假恶丑现象，因而是极具有伦理道德的一个个励志成长的故事。

攻读硕士研究生以后，我阅读最集中的阶段是在作毕业论文那阵子。我的论文是关于唐代诗僧寒山的和合伦理思想，因而这期间，我读了《寒山诗注》《金刚经》《心经》《坛经》《中国禅宗史》等一系列中国传统文化古籍。

说句实话，创作论文这三个月的阅读量简直要赶上整个硕士三年的了。因为我前两年要么是给报刊写稿，要么是进行社会工作，并没有读多少本专业书籍，但这三个月的系统阅读，的确大大开阔了我的佛学与经学视野，令我对佛教寺庙文化的认识提升了许多。

2010年我进入职场，工作后的阅读时间比起学校时期理论上来说是应该少了，但如果我们真要喜欢阅读的话，书本是不会离开我们左右的。我恰是如此，进入社会后反而更珍惜与书本的感情，即便工作再忙，每天不读书，就觉得如同不吃饭血糖要降低一样难受。

也许我这么说夸张了，但如果把阅读变成我们生活习惯的话，在书桌、在床头、在我们任何经常看到方便拿到的生活地方摆上书，那我们的阅读习惯就会逐渐养成。

而对于我恰是如此，毕业后，我喜欢上了逛书店，喜欢上了上网

After entering university, facing a whole library, we are entering the ocean of knowledge! While talking about the reading experience of my undergraduate, now want to be far from the Bookworm's standard, and very point interesting is that I love the martial arts book. My first choice is reading Jin Yong's book, because Jin Yong's concept of many people, his books, film and television are the first martial arts man. "The flying snowflakes shot the white deer, the good man learning mandarin duck" is that I read Jin Yong's works order, and most of them finished.

My experience is that the reason why Mr Jin Yong is receive praise from intellectual, reading circles, civilian circles and all sectors of society, it is because the book is definitely not simple fighting, but full of positive energy,and contain everything, actively promote the traditional culture of "benevolence, righteousness, propriety, wisdom, trust, with good faith, virtue and patriotism and swordsman, criticize false evil and ugliness such as betrayal of faith and abandonment of justics, one inspirational story with great ethics and morality.

After I studied for a master's degree, the most intensive stage of my reading was in my graduation thesis. My thesis is about the Tang Dynasty poem monk Hanshan and ethical thought, so during this period, I read "Han Shan poetry note" "Diamond Sutra" "Heart Sutra" "Altar Sutar" "Chinese Zen history" and a series of China ancient traditional culture ancient books.

To tell you the truth, the amount of reading in the three months of the creative paper almost caught up with the master for three years. Because the last two years I either wrote to journalism, or worked on social work, and did not read many of the professional books, but the three months of systematic reading, indeed greatly broadened my vision of Buddhist classics, raised my understanding of the Buddhist temple culture.

I entered the job market in 2010, and reading hours in work should be less than school period, but if we really wanted to read, the book wouldn't leave us. I was so, after entering society, and more cherish the feelings with books, even if the work is busy, do not read every day, I will feel as uncomfortable as skipping meals and lowering blood sugar.

买书，更是有意或无意的关注历年的"茅盾文学奖""鲁迅文学奖""诺贝尔文学奖"等一系列中外文学奖项，这些作家的作品也就成为我马上或准备阅读的对象。阅读过程中，有时对哪位作家或哪本书籍感兴趣，会去百度百科查阅其相关背景。

如果真的非常喜欢，就会去买来那些作品。我工作这四年来，自己买的加上朋友送的，已经累积有几百本书籍、上千本各类杂志了。前一阵朋友送了我一个书架，我把这些书刊一一排列上去，然后拍照传到朋友圈和腾讯空间，引来各种赞誉。当然，我自己也是极为欣慰，这些图书不光令我的小屋书香盎然，也使得我的精神世界越发充裕。让我深感书籍的伟大，知识的庄严，文化的厚重。

我可以肯定的是，阅读将会伴随我的一生，而我建立的家庭也一定会是书香门第。我愿我的爱人、孩子都喜欢上阅读，愿意所有认识我的人也都爱上阅读。我更希望我的祖国、我生活的这个地球上的所有人都因为有了阅读，而使得人生变得愈发精彩。

载于《文苑》

智慧箴言

阅读是迄今为止我们发现的最好的习惯了，通过阅读，来清晰地认知这个所处的世界和自己。与书对话，就是与自己对话。

May I say so exaggerated, but if we make reading a habit, on the desk, in bed, we often put the book in any convenient place, then we will gradually develop reading habits.

That's exactly what it is, after graduation, I like shopping in bookstores and buying books online, it is deliberate or unintentional focus on the "Mao Dun prize" "Lu Xun prize" "Nobel prize" and a series of Chinese and foreign literary awards, these writers works have become me immediately or ready to read the object. In the process of reading, you are sometimes interested in which author or which book you go to the Baidu encyclopedia to check its related background.

If you really like it, you'll buy those works. During my four years of work, bought by myself and sent by my friends, and I have accumulated hundreds of books and thousands of magazines. A friend sent me a bookshelf, I arranged these books one by one, and then take pictures to the moment and Tencent space, attracting a variety of praise. Of course, I am also very pleased, these books not only make my cabin full of elegant abundant, but also make my spiritual world more abundant. I am deeply aware of the greatness of books, the solemn of knowledge and the depth of culture.

I am sure that reading will be with my life, and I will establish the family will be a scholarly family. I want my lover and children will be like to read, and all the people who know me fall in love with reading. I would prefer that my country and all the people who are on the earth make life more exciting because of reading.

Reading is by far the best habit we have ever discovered. By reading, we can clearly recognize the world and ourselves. Talking to books is talking to yourself.

创业其实就是敢想敢做

文 / 刘进

> 如果他是一棵软弱的芦草，就让他枯萎吧；如果他是一个勇敢的人，就让他自己闯出一条路来吧。
>
> ——司汤达

比尔是美国弗吉尼亚州的一位在校大学生，他的家庭非常富有，父亲有两家公司，母亲是高级法院的律师。但是，当离开家上大学时，他却拒绝了父亲为他准备的一张十万美元的银行卡。临走时，他信心满满地对父亲说："我只需要带点车费就行，上学的费用我自己想办法就可以解决。"他的父母一脸吃惊，但是看到比尔那么自信，只好答应了。

刚到大学，比尔就跑到一家餐厅请求店主，说自己愿意为餐厅送外卖。因为大学里面是不允许开餐厅的，很多餐厅都在学校外面。外面餐厅很多，竞争压力很大，所以店主很快就答应了。并且答应他每销售一份外卖，就能获得一美元提成。

比尔为了提高销售量，获取更多的提成，便用自己仅剩的 20 美元给餐厅印刷广告，然后把全校每个寝室都跑了个遍，发广告做宣传。当天就有人陆续打电话过来订外卖，这是比尔意料之中的。学校寝室距离

Entrepreneur Is Thinker and Doer

If he is a weak weed, let him wither; if he is a brave man, let him pave his own way.

——Stendhal

Bill was a college student in Virginia, United States. He was born in a very rich family: his father owned two companies and his mother was a lawyer of the Supreme Court. However, when he was leaving home for college, he refused a USD 100,000 debit card his father prepared for him. Before he left, he told his father with confidence, "I only need some money to cover my fare. I can get the tuition fees by myself." Astonished by his confidence, Bill's parents agreed him to do so.

The first thing Bill did after he registered at college was to ask for the owner of a restaurant that he would do the deliver job. As restaurants were not allowed on campus, a lot of restaurants opened outside the campus. Since the restaurant competition pressure is high, the owner of that restaurant soon made a deal with Bill, offering him one dollar out of each deliver order.

In order to increase his sales volume and get more commission, he printed leaflets for the restaurant using 20 dollars that was left with him, and advertised with the leaflets to every dormitory on campus. There were some orders for food delivered on that day, as was unexpected. As it

93

外面很远，肯定会有学生不愿意多走路，宁愿多花一点钱。以后的一个月里，外卖销售量迅速增长，比尔从一天拿30美元的提成增长到了每天200美元！

令人意想不到的是，当这份工作做得如火如荼时，比尔居然辞职不干了。他拿着挣来的5000美元，到即将毕业的学长那里收购二手自行车。在学校，有些同学为了方便，买了自行车代替步行。快毕业时，自行车不方便带回家，只能当作垃圾卖掉。比尔正是意识到了这一点，便立即做出了行动，到学长们那里进行宣传称愿意高价回收二手自行车。

大家一看有人愿意高价回收旧自行车，都很愿意把自己骑旧的自行车卖出去。这样一来，比尔很快就收购了几十辆自行车。接下来，他继续发广告，不一样的是，这次他是为自己发广告。原来，他把收购来的自行车修理、刷洗之后，成立了一个自行车出租"公司"。

这次，比尔又抓住了新生们的心理。有很多新生想买自行车，但是平常上课没时间出行，只有周末才骑车出去玩买新的又会觉得浪费，又想到毕业时自行车只能当垃圾卖出去，所以买车时很犹豫。这下一听说有人出租自行车，自然打消了买车的念头。于是，比尔以10美元一天的价格出租自行车，平常每天能租出去20多辆，周末时自行车能够全部出租完。看到自己的"生意"十分火爆，赚到钱后，比尔继续收购自行车，增加出租量。很快，比尔就成了学校里的名人，同学们都称他为"创业天才"。

一年以后，比尔正式成立了出租公司，他花钱请了一些人员，把出租自行车的范围扩展到周围好几家大学，还开了几家自行车店面，出售新自行车。毕业时，他的自行车出租公司和自行车专卖店加起来的销售额已经达到父亲一家公司的销售额！这让父母对他刮目相看。

was pretty far from campus to the restaurants, a number of students were willing to buy food with extra money. In the following month, the delivery orders grew rapidly and Bill got his commission from 30 dollars a day to 200 dollars!

What was unexpected was that Bill quitted his job when it was growing so vigorously. With 5,000 dollars that he earned, Bill made another deal with the seniors to buy their second-hand bicycles. A lot of college students rode bicycles on campus instead of walking and discarded them after they graduated. Being aware of this, Bill launched a campaign among the seniors, saying that he wanted to buy their bicycles with high prices. Students were happy that there was a way to sell their bicycles instead of discarding them. Therefore, Bill bought dozens of second-hand bicycles. Again, he made advertisements, but this time, for himself. It turned out that he started his own "bicycle rent company" after he fixed and cleaned them.

This time, again, Bill grasped the mind of freshmen. Many first-year students hesitated before they decided to buy a new bicycle: they needed a bicycle only when they have time to go for a ride on weekends, and it could be a waste to buy a brand new one, which will be discarded after they graduate. When they knew that there was someone who lent second-hand bicycles, they just threw away the idea of buying new one. Bill, with the rental price of 10 dollars each day, got over 20 bicycles rent every day and all of them rent on weekends. Later on, he started to expand his business by buying more second-hand bicycles with greater investment and increasing the rental of bicycles. Soon, he became a celebrity in the college and people called him a entrepreneurial genius.

A year later, Bill set up his rent company officially. He hired some employees and extended his business to nearby college and universities. He also started shops that sold brand new bicycles. By the time when he graduated, the gross sales of his rent company and bicycle shops had reached the total gross sales of one of his father's companies! This refreshed his image in his parents' mind.

当有人问到比尔创业的感受时，比尔答道："我就是一个普通的大学生，能走到今天，只不过是比别人多了一点敢想敢做的勇气而已。"

当年已经 46 岁的乔布斯，在自己的事业里依然坚持敢想敢做的个性。他推出了苹果音乐播放器，带动了全球 mp3 的疯狂流行，又具有前瞻性地把苹果带到了手机和个人电脑行业。短短 10 年的时间，乔布斯的敢想敢做，让苹果公司变成了庞大的帝国！

李开复也曾说过："人生在世的时间非常短暂，如果你总是不敢做想做的事情，那么一生过去了，你留下来的只有悔恨、懊恼。我常常说追随我心，冒一些风险是值得的。"

因为敢想，所以梦想一直都在眼前；因为敢做，所以成功并不遥远。这两个可以成就人生的词，我们应该把它们当作人生的信条。

载于《当代青年》

智 慧 箴 言

做任何事都需要十足的勇气，没有勇气就克服不了困难，没有勇气就改正不了错误，没有勇气就取得不了成功。在我们的学习、生活、工作中，勇气是至关重要的。

When asked about the secret of success, Bill said, "I am an ordinary college student, I can go to this day, just a little more courage than other people dare to do."

Steve Jobs insisted on his personality of being a thinker and doer at the age of 46. He released iPod, driving people to be crazy about the mp3. And he led Apple into mobile phone and computer industry prospectively. Within a decade, Jobs made Apple as an enormous empire!

Li Kai-fu once said, "Life is very short, and if you dare not to do what you want, your life will end up with regret, remorse and anger. I tell myself to do whatever I want, and it is worth taking some risk. "

Think about your dream and take actions to succeed. These words can be taken as a belief of life.

Everything needs courage. Without courage, we won't overcome difficulties; without courage, we won't achieve success. Courage is vital in our life, work and study.

锁不住的财富之门

文 / 梅若雪

> 不要对一切人都以不信任的眼光看待，但要谨慎
> 而坚定。
>
> ——德谟克里特

"海东明月锁光阴，花在月中心。"与其让朗朗明月锁住一份美好的光阴，毋宁让自己变得更有创意，让人生在月光中开出一朵鲜艳美丽的花来。

荷娜·金从美国著名的杜克大学毕业后，在一家投资银行做分析师。在下班后一个人的时光里，她往往会坐在寝室的窗前摆弄智能手机。那天晚上，她一次又一次用手指滑动着打开锁着的面板进入界面，一遍遍重复枯燥的动作，她哑然失笑：这单调枯燥的动作已花去了自己多少时间！

突然，一个念头如同窗外的月光点亮了她的思想：时间从来都是创意的最好载体，如果把广告投放到从点亮手机与滑动解锁之间的面板上，这该是多好的商机啊！

当她兴奋地把这一个想法告诉一位同窗好友时，对方却说，如今广告铺天盖地，它们严重污染着人们的视觉，你要是做一个屏蔽广

Unchained Door of Wealth

Don't treat people with distrustful mind, Be prudent and firm.

——Democritus

"Moon lights and sea locks time and blossom in the center of the moon." Instead of wasting the time, one should always be creative and let his life blossom in the moonlight.

After graduation from Duke University, Hana Kim worked as an analyst in an investment bank. She often sits in front of the window of the bedroom to play with her smart phone after work. One night, as she slid and unlocked the phone and entered the home page again and again, she realized that she had wasted a lot of time on this dull repetition!

Suddenly, an idea came to her mind like the luminous moonlight: Time is always the best carrier of creativity, and if I place ads on the interface when people unlock the phone, that is business!

When she told one of her school friends her thoughts, her friend said, people are so exposed to the overwhelming ads, and if you develop an ad-block app, you may establish a market. Hana Kim was then convinced by her friend, and said, "Exactly. There is nothing wrong

告的东西，也许还会有些市场。荷娜·金一听，认为好友的话不无道理，她对好友说："是的，时间本身是没有错的，关键是要做出正确的选择。"

两人经过多次思想交锋和碰撞，一种极具创意的方案终于形成：让受众看广告得报酬。用户点亮智能手机后，无论其是否看了广告，只要他打开了有广告的界面，就可以得到 1 美分的报酬。在一小时内，最多可以获得 3 美分报酬的机会。

细心的人要是算一下账，一小时 3 美分，一天按十小时计算，每天就可得到 30 美分，一年 365 天，则可以得到 109.5 美分，折合人民币 666 元，钱虽然不算多，但它毕竟是一种新玩法、新体验。再说，没有广告不也照样要点亮面板，它并没有给人造成额外负担啊。

当用户积够 10 美分时，便可以对这钱选择性地处理，比如，用户可以用账户中的钱购买礼物卡，也可以兑换成商家的优惠券，还可作为一笔善款捐助给慈善机构，享受做好事的一份满足与快乐。当然，用户还可以通过国际贸易支付工具"贝宝宝"提取现金，让自己的腰包一点点儿"鼓起来"。

也许有人会说，不管给我多大好处，都会对广告有着条件反射性的排斥。这个好办，选择权依然在你手中，荷娜·金和她的团队将其设计成了可向左可向右滑动，任由你处置。如手指头向左滑动时，解锁界面就是广告信息及画面；而向右滑动时，则可避开广告，直接进入手机主界面。

2013 年 3 月，荷娜·金要让她和朋友，还有用户来锁定各自的财富了：她和两位好友注册了名为"Loc Ket"的公司，投身到"锁屏广告"营运上来。很快，Loc Ket 就与 8 家广告商签订了广告投放协议书，其中包括两家"世界 500 强"企业。

为了真正体现"抢占受众注意力"的经营理念，她正努力做到一把

with time. The point is to make the right choice."

After a long time brainstorming, they came up with a creative proposal: Pay the users for watching ads. As long as the users tap to turn on their phone, they can get paid for 1 cent, and they can get 3 cents maximum within an hour.

If one did the math, 3 cents an hour multiplied by 10 hours a day would be 30 cents and multiplied by 365 days a year would be 109.5 cents, the equivalent of 666 RMB. Although it didn't help a person become rich, it was totally a kind of new experience for the users. Anyway, people turned on their phones whether there was an ad or not, so the ads didn't bother them at all.

When a user gathered 10 cents, there were several options for him. For example, a user could use the money in his account to buy present cards or change into coupons, or he could enjoy doing good things through charitable donations. Of course, users could withdraw the money through a payment of international trade and got "richer".

Some might say that they had conditioned reflex rejection on ads no matter how much benefits they got. This is not a big issue as the choice is still yours. Hana Kim and her development team designed that users could swipe the screen left or right, leave it to you. If you swiped left, the ads would enter the unlock screen; and if you swiped right you could skip the ads and enter directly to the home screen.

Since March 2013, Hana Kim would let her friends, the users and herself lock their own fortune: they registered their company "Loc Ket" and devoted themselves to the operation of "lock-screen ads". Soon, Loc Ket signed advertisements placement agreements with eight advertising companies, including two from the Global 500.

In order to implement their management philosophy of "seizing the

钥匙开一把锁。荷娜·金和她的团队通过分析用户的社交网络数据，有针对性地向用户提供优质的广告内容，即根据用户的年龄、性别、地理位置以及参与锁屏广告的黏度等信息，进行精准投放，最终让广告成为精美、看起来并不像广告的艺术享受。

有人看到的只是一把锁，而对于一个有心人来说，看到的却是锁背后的门。只要用自己的创意之钥打开这扇门，你就能进入成功与财富的殿堂。

载于《当代青年》

智 慧 箴 言

只要有勇于发现的心灵，创意就无处不在。如果在一件事物面前更具备一些耐心，你就有可能会发现机遇。

attention of the users", Kim tried to get okay to open a lock. With her friend and the team, they precisely offered ads with good quality through the analyses of users' social media data, such as age, gender, location and participation, and eventually made ads as an artistic enjoyment.

Some people see a lock while a considerate people see the door. One can achieve success and fortune only if he opens the door with creativity.

Be bold enough to explore, and creativity is everywhere. If you can act with more patience, you may find opportunities.

"死"了五万次的人

文 / 汤小小

> 要从容地着手去做一件事，但一旦开始，就要坚持到底。
>
> ——比阿斯

15 岁时，他初涉影视圈，很幸运地得到了一次出演的机会，饰演一个被武士一刀劈死的坏蛋，只有几秒钟的镜头。

为了这几秒钟的镜头，他把剧本从头到尾地看了一遍，虽然自己饰演的角色只被编剧一笔带过，但他还是根据剧情，琢磨出这个人物的性格和与武士打斗时的心态，根据这些，再推理出被杀死时的表情和动作。

因为准备充分，这个镜头一次就拍摄成功，这给了他极大的鼓励。也因为这次的成功，让导演记住了他，以后再有这样的角色，就会第一个找到他。

这样，他又得到了几次出演的机会，虽然每一次呈现给观众的都是被杀死时的几秒钟，但他每一次都不敢有丝毫马虎。剧情不同，人物

The Man Who "died" 50 Thousand Times

Undertake a career calmly. Once started, hold out to the end.

——Beas

When he began his movie career at the age of 15, he was lucky enough to have a chance to play a villain who was hacked to death with one slash by a samurai. The shot took only a few seconds.

For a shot of a few seconds like this, he read through the script from the very beginning to the end. Although the role he was about to play did not have last of description, he worked hard to think about the character's personality and his mentality in the fight against the samurai according to the plots. Based on these efforts, he reasoned out the facial expression and movements the role had before he was killed.

Thanks to the thorough preparation, the shooting succeeded at first attempt, which was a big encouragement for him. His success also left a good impression on the director. Since then, whenever there was a similar role, the director would contact him in the first place.

Consequently, he got several other chances to play. They were all dying scenes of a few seconds, but he never slacked off. Considering that different plots and characters required different styles of deaths, he would read through the scripts carefully each time and designed different manners

不同，死时的状态当然也应该不同。每一次，他都认真看剧本，根据当时的情景，设计出不同的死亡方式。有时是翻白眼，有时是慢慢跪下，有时是狂喊大叫，有时是吐血而亡。

他自创的神态各异的死法，吸引了很多导演和演员的注意。慢慢地，找他拍戏的人越来越多，每一次，都是扮演被杀的角色。

随着"死亡"次数的增加，他慢慢有了一些知名度，很多人劝他，不要再演那种无足轻重的角色了，应该尝试转型，要求导演加戏，争取多露会儿脸，从几秒钟到几分钟，再到重要的配角，最后做主角。

他却摇摇头，人人都去做主角，那坏蛋谁来演呢？演好坏蛋也是一门学问啊！演得好，就能衬托主角的英勇，提升整部戏的品质。

别的演员有接不到戏的时候，他却平均每天都要跑三个剧组，这么忙碌又演得轻车熟路，按说他只要往镜头前一站，随便做个死亡的动作，几秒钟就能拿到劳务费走人了。可是，他却对每一个角色都不肯马虎，总是不断地创造出新的死法。

除了那些传统的死法，他又发明了虾米式死法，把身体弯成一只虾，一伸一缩，不停地抽搐；还发明了搞笑怪诞式死法，在倒下的瞬间，做一些搞笑怪诞的表情和动作。

这样的角色，他一演就是50年，算起来，他在屏幕上总共"死"了五万多次。而这五万次的"死亡"，把他锻造成一个顶级的特技演员，得到观众的喜爱，得到同事的尊重，得到导演的称赞。

他的名字叫福本生三，在光怪陆离的娱乐圈，因饰演被杀的角色而成为知名演员。以最无足轻重的角色而赢得尊重，不能不说这是一个奇迹。

of deaths according to the plot, such as rolling his eyes, kneeling down slowly, screaming or vomiting blood.

His self-created way of death had attracted plenty of directors and actors. Gradually, more and more people would like to invite him to act, and every time, play a role to be killed.

As be "died" for an increasing number of times, he gained reputation gradually. Many people had tried to persuade him that he should give up these insignificant roles for a transition, that he should negotiate with the director for longer scenes, from a few seconds to a few minutes, and then he could became an important supporting actor, and finally, a protagonist.

But he rejected. If everyone was going to be the protagonist, who was there to play the villain? How to play a villain well required knowledge. If he played well, he could foil the courage of the hero and improve the quality of the whole film.

When other actors had no roles to play, he had to play for three different films per day on average. Normally, given such a busy schedule and familiarity with the roles, he only had to stand in front of the camera, made several movements, and after a few seconds, he would get the money and leave. However, he would not relax his efforts on any of these characters, and kept on creating new ways of death.

In addition to those traditional ways of death, he had created shrimp-shaped death, bent his body in a shape of a shrimp and kept jiggling and twitching. Moreover, he had created funny weird ways of death as well, he show up funny looks and posed weird gestures when falling down.

He had played this type of role for 50 years, and devoted 50 thousand times of screen "death". These 50 thousand times made him a top actor and gained popularity from the the audience, he gained respect form colleagues and praise from directors.

He is Seizo Fukumoto, a well-known actor famous for to-be-killed roles in the bizarre world of entertainment. It is a miracle that he gains respect for playing the most insignificant role.

And what made the miracle happened were 50 years of persistence

而创造这个奇迹的，是五十年如一日的坚持，是认真对待每一个角色的职业操守。无论多么微小的事情，只要认真坚持去做，就会创造奇迹。

载于《意林》

智 慧 箴 言

　　追梦路上，坎坷丛生，会有很多的迷茫，未来遥遥无期，不知道该去往哪里。既然不知道去往哪里，那我们不如就过好每一天。其实，根本没有什么所谓的更好的路，你选择的那一条，只要坚持走，就是最好的路。好多年以后迷茫的人依旧迷茫，可你已经脱胎换骨。所以，你只要做好自己，其他的上天自有安排。

and work ethics of taking every role seriously. No matter how trivial a thing is, once you devoted your efforts and persistence to it, you will create miracles.

The road to dream was bumpy and confusing The future seems so far away, leaving you confused about where to go. Since you can not see a destination, why not live your life to its fullest every day. In fact, there is no better way. The way you choose is the best way as long as you persist to it. Many years later, when confused people remain confused, you have completely reshaped yourself. Therefore, you need to be yourself, and let the God plan the rest.

在"岔路"上找回自信

文 / 嵇振颉

> 不要失去信心，只要坚持不懈，就终会有成果的。
>
> ——钱学森

2008 年高考，他以 660 多分青海省理科第五名的成绩，被北京大学生命科学学院录取。

入学前，他觉得生命科学是交叉学科，未来的职业前景一定不错。可是，一切似乎都朝着他设想之外的方向运行，专业课枯燥乏味，让他感到很不适应。他不想成为只会搞理论的学究，这不是他想要的生活。

他想换个专业，由于成绩不够只能作罢，于是，他开始放纵自己，在网络游戏中醉生梦死。通宵"练级""做任务"，他因此生了一场大病，不得不暂时休学回家静养。身体稍微好一点，他又决定利用这段空闲时间到社会上"闯荡"一下。他当过电话接线员、做过流水线工人，因为没有一技之长，又不擅长交际，只能干这些没有技术含量的工作。休学期满，他辞去工作，再次回到宁静的校园，希望重新找回自信。

Get Confidence Back on the "Wrong" Road

Don't lose confidence. As long as you persist in doing it, you will eventually succeed.

——Qian Xuesen

In 2008, he passed the College Entrance Examination and got admitted to School of Life Science of Peking University with more than 660 points ranking the 5th among all science students in Qinghai province.

Before enrollment, he was expecting a bright future career prospect since life science was an interdisciplinary subject. But it seemed that everything was going beyond his expectation. He could not adapt himself to the tediousness of the courses, nor did he want to become a pedant who knew researches and theories only. It was not the life that he wanted.

He had attempted to change his major, but failed because of the insufficient GPA. Therefore, he began to abandon himself to online games. Nights after nights he drowned in improving levels and finishing tasks in games, then he fell seriously ill and had to suspend his schooling and return home for a rest. When he felt better, he decided to spend this free time to expose himself to the society. He had worked as a telephone operator and an assembly-line worker. Since he did not have professional skills and was not good at communication, he could only do simple work that did not require skills. When the suspension was expired, he quit the job, and returned to school, hoping find his confidence back.

可是，现实再次泼了他一盆冷水，他对未来越来越迷茫。就在此时，朋友邀请他参观就读的北京工业技师学院。在学院的课堂上，学习内容不再只是枯燥的理论，来自生产第一线的老师傅，手把手地向他们传授积累了几十年的经验。他被眼前的景象深深吸引，一个念头在心里萌发：从北大退学，到这所技师学院学习。

"什么？你要从北大退学，去一个从来没听说过的学校？你是不是疯了？"很多人对他的想法表示难以置信，父亲在电话里和他吵了好几架，气得撂下几句话："技校是什么地方？那是读书不好的人才去的地儿。你这个高才生去那里读书，不是大材小用吗？如果不听我的话，以后有你后悔的。"

他不会改变自己的想法，他决定先说服母亲。听到儿子的决定，母亲也很震惊。不过想到儿子在北大读书的痛苦经历，做娘的心还是软了下来：与其让孩子一天到晚生活在苦恼中，还不如顺着他的兴趣尝试新的道路。终于，在母亲的劝说下父亲同意了他的决定。

2011年冬天，他来到北京工业技师学院求学。考虑到他有一定的理论基础，学校让他直接进入技师班学习，并给他配了最好的班主任。他终于有机会近距离地接触到十几台从瑞士进口的数控机器了，为了赶上大家的进度，他学得格外认真：总是第一个来到实验室，一待就是好几个小时，常常连饭也忘了吃。直到实验室管理员在一旁催促，他才恋恋不舍地离开。

他的努力没有白费，凭借北大的理论基础和北京工业技师学院的技术学习，他成为学院优秀的学生之一。2014年11月，第六届全国数控技能大赛决赛开幕式在北京工业技师学院举行。会场上，他代表参赛选手进行宣誓。比赛中，他的一招一式都显得那么娴熟，最终夺得数控技能大赛第一名。好多企业向这位行业技能高手伸出橄榄枝，他用成绩

However, the reality once again failed him. He became increasingly confused about the future. At that time, his friend invited him to visit Beijing Industrial Technician College. He found that students there did not learn tedious theories in classes. Instead, there were masters craftsmen from forefront production lines passing on their experience that was accumulated for decades to students, hand in hand. He was deeply impressed by this, an idea came to him: Drop out from Peking University and study here.

"What? You want to quit Peking University and go to that unknown school? Are you insane?" Many people could not understand what he was thinking. His father had argued with him several times through telephone, and threatened, "Do you have any idea about a vocational school? It's a place where bad students go. You are a top student, don't you think you are wasting your talent there? You will regret it if you do not listen to me."

He wound not change his mind, and decided to persuade his mother first. On hearing her son's decision, the mother was shocked, too. However, thinking about the painful experience her son had gone through at Peking University, she finally yielded: It would be better for her son to try new things following his interest rather than live in pain all day long at Peking University. Eventually, his mother had persuaded his father to agree on his decision.

In the winter of 2011, he came to Beijing Industrial Technician College for study. Considering that he had already had certain theoretical basis, the school let him study in technician classes directly, and gave him the best teacher. He finally got the chance to have a close contact with dozens of numerically controlled machines imported from Switzerland. In order to catch up with his classmates, he studied extremely hard: He was always the first one to come to the laboratory, and stay there for hours, often forgot to eat. Furthermore, he would not leave until the lab assistant urged him to.

His efforts had paid off. By virtue of his theoretical background cultivated at Peking University plus the practical skills learned at Beijing Industrial Technician College, he became one of the best students in the college. In November 2014, the opening ceremony of the finals of the Sixth National Game of NC Technique was held at Beijing Industrial Technician College, and he took the oath on behalf of contestants. In the

证明曾说过的话："如果一辈子都做自己不喜欢的事，你的一生就毁了。"

他叫周浩，是一名从北大退学的在读的技校生，面对媒体采访，他自信地说："我所学的技术在生活中起着很大的作用，我不会后悔自己的选择。三百六十行，行行出状元，每个人只要在适合自己、自己感兴趣的岗位上工作，都会变得强大的！"

正如乔布斯所说："你必须要找到你所爱的东西。"在别人认为的"岔路"上，周浩找回了自信，找到了他所热爱的事业，由此成就了精彩人生。

智 慧 箴 言

> 每个人都是独一无二的，每个人都应该去寻找那个最真的自己，做自己最喜欢的工作，努力成为想成为的那种人。就像村上春树说的那般贴切："你要听话，去过自己另外的生活，不是所有的鱼都生活在同一片海里。"

contest, he was skilled in every aspect and eventually won the first prize. Many companies offered their positions to this skilled technician, and he approved what he had said by achievements, "If you devote your whole life to things you don't like, your life will be ruined."

He is Zhou Hao, an enrolled technical school student and a dropped-out student from Peking University. "The techniques I learned play a significant role in my life, and I do not regret my choice. Every profession has its master. As long as you find out what is suitable for you and you have interest in it, you will be strong!" He told the media confidently.

As Steve Jobs had said, " You've to find what you love." On what others believed was a wrong path, Hao got his confidence back and found the career he loved, thus winning a wonderful life.

Everyone is unique. One should find the real self, do what you like and strive to be what you want to be. Just as said properly by Murakami Haruki, "you have to listen to your heart and live a different life, as not all fishes are living in one ocean."

寻找探寻的眼睛

文 / 清翔

> 我的人生哲学是工作，我要揭示大自然的奥妙，为人类造福。
>
> ——爱迪生

张文学最初创业一连失利，那年，无比苦闷的他只身来到阿拉善，在别人的带领下他到了大漠深处的一个地方。在一片苍茫的黄沙之中，他竟然发现一片似点缀着宝石一样的湖水，四周芦苇飘荡，湖中野鸭成群，有天鹅正引颈歌唱着……他的心灵不禁受到极大的震撼。

原来，这颗"宝石"就是月亮湖。正被开发着，要让她成为极富视觉和心灵冲击力的旅游胜地。在见到开发者的那一瞬，张文学心中蓦然跳出一个问题：你是怎么发现这个地方的？又何以想到要开发它？

对方的一句话顿时让他心中明亮清澈起来……

时间的脚步到了 2007 年，一个炎热的午后，印度东部沙漠腹地的一个小镇，突然狂风大作，满眼的沙子，还有马粪，甚或不小的石子在空中飞舞着。此时已是基伍国际有限公司董事长兼总经理的张文学在那里公干，在当地他见到一件奇特的事正进行着：许多当地人在一辆后座

Seek For Eyes of Exploration

My philosophy of life is work, I want to reveal
the mysteries of nature, for the benefit of mankind.

——Edison

When he started business at the beginning, Zhang Wenxue failed
again and again. In that year, upset and depressed, under the guidance of
others, he came to Alashan and reached a location deep in the desert where
he found a lake in the boundless sand like a diamond. Reeds drifting all
around with groups of wild ducks swimming on the lake and swan singing,
all these were vibrating in his mind.

In fact, this "diamond" is the Moon Lake, which was under construction
into an enchanting and inspirational tourist resort. At the moment when he
met the developer, two questions suddenly occurred to him: how did you
find this place? And why did you exploit it?

The developer's response swept away his confusions…

Time flashes to the year 2007. In a scorching afternoon, a storm
suddenly stroke a small town in the hinterland of a desert in eastern India
and sands, horseshit and even big stones were flying in the sky. Zhang
Wenxue, the current president and general manager of Jiwu International
Co., Ltd. was also on business there. He saw an interesting phenomenon:
many local people were queuing beside a bike with an automobile storage
battery on the back seat. These people were charging their phones. Ten

117

上绑着汽车蓄电池的自行车旁边排着长队——这些人是在给手机充电，人们交 10 卢比（约 1.3 元人民币），就可以在蓄电池上充电半小时。张文学用眼睛骨碌碌地看着这些人，人们也拿眼睛看着他，他的心怦然一动。

几个月后，张文学就开始在印度销售一款配有超大容量电池的手机，待机时间长达 30 天。

原来，印度东部人在沙漠中一走就是好多天，即便遇到一些小镇，由于没有电力设施，电池早已耗尽的手机也不能充电。当地那些头脑灵活的人，就开始利用这种难得的商机做生意。

而基伍的大容量电池让印度这些东部人如获至宝，其配有大容量电池的手机在印度市场出货量一年高达 3500 万部，占有率 21%，遥遥领先排名第二的诺基亚。

自从到月亮湖之后，张文学就经常进入沙漠的深处，就连迪拜这些国家，他每年至少去 6 次，每次都会背上背囊，在沙漠的一些角角落落行走上一周。

那天，张文学搭了当地人的一辆汽车去参加一次活动，原来，迪拜人最热衷的消遣地并非酒吧、KTV，而是举家驱车前往沙漠深处烧烤。到了目的地后，见到的只是一片黄色及流线体，为了打破这种单调，他们便以音乐来烘托气氛。可人们不是携带老式录音机，就是发动汽车使用汽车音响。那天，当地的这位朋友不知是想节约一点汽油，还是忘了发动汽车，就打开音响，一边烧烤，一边载歌载舞起来。

然而，当晚上月亮升起，寒气袭来，淋漓酣畅玩了一天的他们要回家时，汽车却不能发动了。因为电池已被耗光了，大家不得不一起推车发动汽车。

rupees (or 1.3 yuan) will allow for charging for 0.5 hour. When he was staring at these people who were also looking at them, an idea emerged in his mind.

Months later, Zhang Wenxue began to sell mobile phones with large battery capacity with standby time of 30 days.

Actually, it takes several days for people to go through a desert in eastern India. Even though they may encounter some small towns, it is impossible to charge their phones running out of electricity due to the lack of power facilities. Therefore smart local people are securing this precious business opportunity.

Batteries with large capacity offered by Jiwu were also regarded as treasure in the eyes of local people. 35 million mobile phones with these batteries were sold annually in India, accounting for 21% of the market share, far ahead of Nokia ranked the 2nd place.

Since he went to the Moon Lake, Zhang Wenxue has often enter deep places in desert. He goes to Dibai, such a small country, for at least 6 times a year. Whenever he goes, he will pack his bags and spend a week walking in different corners of the desert.

On that day, he took a car of a local people to take part in an activity. It turned out that the favorite recreation of local people in Dubai was not bars or KTVs, but to drive to a place deep in the desert for barbecue. When he arrived, all he saw was streamlined bare yellow sand. To break this monotony, they used music to create a favorable ambience. But they either use old recorders or vehicle's stereo system. On that day, the local friend may either want to save gasoline or forget to start the car. He just turned on the audio, barbecuing while singing and dancing.

The moon rose in the evening and coldness swept over. Exhausted, they decided to go back home after a day's entertainment. However, they failed to start the car running down the battery. Therefore, all of them had to push the car to start it.

This embarrassing experience inspired him again and Jiwu began to integrate speakers into phones. Four months later, this product was popular

这次尴尬的经历又一次激发了张文学的灵感，基伍公司开始将大喇叭整合进手机。四个月后，他们推出的大喇叭手机受到了迪拜当地人的热捧，此类产品的销量很快高达 800 万部，净利润高达 20%。

　　当有人问起张文学为什么总往沙漠深处跑时，他说，当年我到月亮湖时，是开发月亮湖老板的一句话让我如醍醐灌顶，老板说："人们说月亮湖是沙漠的眼睛，当你在寻找沙漠的眼睛时，沙漠的眼睛也在探寻着世上有眼光的人。"

　　从此，张文学开始做最为深入的市场调查，哪怕是炎热且又随时狂风怒号、飞沙走石的印度沙漠腹地他也经常到访。由此，他对不同市场的需求特点了如指掌。

　　对市场的熟稔形成了对市场极为快速的反应，基伍能在 40 天内为印度开发定制产品，而诺基亚开发一种产品则至少需要 18 个月。特别是那些一般的新手机，基伍每周都要推出 2 款。在基伍的产品展厅中，你可以找到双电池、能插 4 张 SIM 卡、类比电视等不同机种。目前，基伍在市场流通的手机款式总数在 200 个左右。

　　而且基伍产品价格也是最低的，如诺基亚在印度推出的 X2、O2 的音乐手机，其零售价超过 500 元人民币，而基伍的类似产品售价不超过 300 元，电池却比诺基亚的大，支持前后左右摄像头。

　　从 2008 年以来，基伍的产品成功销往印度、东南亚、中东、非洲及南美洲等新兴市场，其中约有四成销往印度及巴基斯坦。在印度的销量，其市场占有率世界排名第二；其 GLX 品牌手机销往巴基斯坦，世界排名第一。基伍公司月出口手机 300 万台，年销售额 70 亿元，并力争三年之内成为全球手机行业前三名。

　　寻找探寻的眼睛，就是关注消费者最为迫切的需求。只有当你不

in Dubai its sales reached 8 million and a net profit of 20%.

When someone asked Zhang Wenxue why he always go to places deep in desert, he said, when I went to the Moon Lake, it was the developer of the Lake that enlightened me. The boss said, "People say that the Moon Lake is the desert's eyes, when you are looking for the eyes of the desert, its eyes are also looking for people who have vision."

Since then, Zhang Wenxue began to conduct the most in-depth market research, even in the hot hinterland of India where storms and blown sands may occur at any time. As a result, he became well aware of the different needs of the different markets.

Familiarity with the market has created a very rapid response to the market, which enabled Jiwu to develop customized products for India within 40 days. In comparison, it took at least 18 months for Nokia to produce the same type of the product.In particular, Jiwu will launch two types of those generally new mobile phones each week. In Jiwu's showroom, you can even find phones with two batteris, phones that can be inserted with 4 SIM cards,or those analogous to TVs. At present, there is a total of 200 models circulating in the market.

Prices of Jiwu's products were also the lowest. For instance, X2 and O2 music phones launched by Nokia in India were priced at over 500 yuan but the price of similar products of Jiwu was less than 300 yuan, their furthermore, battery is much larger with all-round cameras.

Since 2008, Jiwu's products have been successfully exported to India, Southeast Asia, the Middle East, Africa and South America and other emerging markets, of which about fourty percent were sold to India and Pakistan. Sales in India accounted for the second largest market share of the world; its GLX brand mobile phones sold in Pakistane predominated the world market. Monthly export of mobile phones was three million with annual sales of 7 billion yuan. The company was striving to be listed among the top three in the mobile phone industry.

Seeking for the eyes of exploration is to pay attention to the urgent needs of consumers. As long as you are not afraid of difficulties and able to

怕困难，能够做最深入的调查研究，全身心地寻找他人内心的指向时，别人就会和你心心相印，你也就找到了一条宽广的事业之道。

载于《山东青年》

智慧箴言

　　生活不是缺少美，只是缺少发现美的眼睛。这句话放在创业中也是合适的，一双探寻的眼睛，往往更容易发现洞藏的商机，利益因此而来！

make in-depth research to find out people's needs, your supply will match with demand so that a broad career path will appear in front of you.

There is beauty in life. What lacks are eyes that can find beauty. This is also appropriate when it comes to business. Eyes of exploration will be more likely to find out the hidden buisness opportunities that generate great profits!

像做蛋糕一样做事业

文 / 郑亚琼

> 一滴水只有放进大海里才永远不会干涸，一个人只有当他把自己和集体事业融合在一起的时候才能最有力量。
>
> ——雷锋

夏里峰是 PPTV 早期创业团队的成员，后因工作去深圳待了一段时间，再回来的时候发现视频领域发展迅速，已经不适合创业了。

一个偶然的机会，夏里峰加入武汉奇米网络科技有限公司，开始了在电子商务领域的创业之旅。

对于做导购，夏里峰有自己的想法，以网络作为一个有效的平台玩转流量，对于网购如此火爆的今天，是比较容易生存的。但是这样的网站已经不少了，像瀑布流、蘑菇街、美丽说都是类似杂志的风格，具有"高大上"的品风，而自己的网站应该以什么样的形象面众才能赢得更多的顾客呢？自己又如何能在众多导购网站中树立自己的品牌形象呢？

那一段时间里，这些问题一直困扰着夏里峰。一次出差，夏里峰

Run Your Business as Making A Cake

A drop of water will not dry up only it is put into the sea. A man is most powerful when he integrates himself into the collective objective.

——Lei Feng

Xia Lifeng is a member of the early entrepreneurial team of PPTV. After staying in Shenzhen for working reasons, when he came back, he found it was unsuitable for him to start business in the rapidly developed field of video.

By accident, he joined Wuhan Qimi Online Sci-Tech Co., Ltd. and began his journey in e-commerce.

He had his own ideas about developing a shopping guide. It is easy to survive the market to use the Internet as an effective platform to secure network flows against the context of the popular online shopping. But there are many similar sites, like Pinterest, Mushroom Street and Beauty Talk. They all have similar features of magazines targeting high-end consumers. How could he characterize his site to win more consumers? And how to build his brand image among so many sites that offers guidance on shopping?

During that period, these questions perplexed him all the time. On one business trip, Xia Lifeng stayed at a hotel in a town. When he passed over a business street of a community in the morning, which was not prosperous,

住在一个县城的宾馆里，早上办事的时候经过一个社区的商业街，那条商业街并不繁华，奇怪的是一家名叫"一分利蛋糕店"里的顾客却络绎不绝。

到了晚上，夏里峰办完事，又经过蛋糕店，正好店主在收拾东西，准备打烊，夏里峰借机和店主攀谈起来。店主是一对面善的中年夫妻，谈到当初创业的情景，妻子显得相当激动："当初我们夫妻双双下岗，因为他的祖辈曾在御膳房里做过面点，所以他想开个蛋糕店。可是，怎么才能让蛋糕适合大众的口味，他还是下了一番功夫。那段时间，他天天做蛋糕、点心，做完了就送到敬老院给老人免费品尝，让大家给他提意见。社区里跳舞的老年人、玩游戏的小孩、谈朋友的小青年，没有一个没吃过我们老杨做的蛋糕的。"

妻子说到这里的时候，老杨在一旁憨憨地笑，他说："我一次一次地尝试，只想根据不同年龄段，做出各种大家喜欢吃的蛋糕而已。"

这时，妻子的脸上露出了骄傲的神情。"这倒是，功夫不负有心人，我们开店之前，大家见了我俩都说，你们开店吧，蛋糕做得这么好吃，开了店我们一定捧场，免费给你们做宣传。"

夏里峰不禁为夫妻俩竖起了大拇指，拜别他们，他心里豁然开朗。要做市场，必须找准定位，走时尚风或许利润更大，但是却引不起大众的兴趣。只有走大众路线，选择优质商品把价格压到最低，才能获得好口碑。就像夫妻俩的蛋糕店一样，有了好口碑就不愁没有顾客。

不久后，在夏里峰的努力下，建立了卷皮网，并获得 5000 万 A 轮融资。网上开辟了服装、鞋包、母婴、居家等众多子频道，所有的商品均在 200 元以下，折扣降到最低，并设置卷皮返利一项，最高可获得 50% 的商品返利。卷皮网的宗旨就是让顾客"更省钱、更省力、更省心"。

he noticed a strange scene that consumers came in a continuous stream to a store called "One-Cent-Profit Cake Shop".

In the evening, when he finished his business and passed by the shop again, he found the owner was preparing to end a day's business. Xia Lifeng took the opportunity to talk with the owner—a kind couple. Talking about the time when they started business, the wife was quite excited, "at that time, we were just made redundant. Since his ancestors once made pastries for the emperor, he decided to set up a cake shop. He made an effort to develop a popular taste. During that time, he made cakes and desserts every day and sent them to the elder people in nursing home without charges so as to get their comments. All the old people who dance in the community, children playing games or young couples have tasted my husband's cakes."

When his wife said that, Lao Yang (her husband) smiled kindly, saying, "I tried again and again just to find a popular taste that satisfy the appetite of people at different ages."

With pride on her face, the wife said, "That is true. God helps those who help themselves. Before we started our business, all the people had suggested us to open a store as the cake was really delicious, saying that they would publicize for our store freely and buy our cakes."

Xia Lifeng was so adored of them that he turned up the thumb unconsciously and an idea emerged in his mind. Effective marketing requires precise positioning. Fashion-oriented guidance may be more profitable but it cannot attract the mass public. Reputation results from a mass route and quality products with the lowest price. Just as this cake shop, a good reputation will make it unnecessary to worry about customers.

Shortly after, Xia Lifeng set up Juanpi Net with great efforts and acquired 50million yuan at the first round of financing. He created sub-channels, such as clothing, shoes and bags, infant & mom, home products, etc., and all the products are priced below 200 yuan with the greatest discount. An option of Juanpi Profit-return is also developed by which customers can get a discount as high as 50%. The purpose of Juanpi Net is to "save more money, offer quality products and bring more convenience" to consumers.

就这样，卷皮网渐渐被网购者熟知，成了网购者真正的朋友。在给新的创业团队分享心得时，夏里峰却连连表示自己并不算成功的创业者，自己只是在"像做蛋糕一样做事业"。众人疑惑其中的奥秘，夏里峰笑着说，创业确实要多花心思，有时候成功的奥秘只是在不起眼的一个角落里，需要你去发现、领悟。

载于《初中生之友》

智 慧 箴 言

　　记得很久前的一个广告："大家好，才是真的好。"它言简意赅地说明，市场的定义是面向大众的。我们要学会用大众的眼光看待问题，这样，才能将利益最大化。

In this way, Juanpi Net becomes a widely known name and a true friend of online shoppers. When sharing experience with new start-ups, Xia Lifeng always refuses to call himself a successful entrepreneur but says that he is just "running his business like making a cake". When people are confused, he responds with a smile that it takes great effort to start a business. Sometimes, the secret of success is just in a nameless corner that needs to be discovered and understood.

Long time ago, there is an ad, "Everybody is good is really good." To put it simple, market is designed to be people-oriented. We have to understand a question from the eyes of the public so that profits will be maximized.

我之所爱为我天职

文 / 纳兰泽芸

不能爱哪行才干哪行，要干哪行爱哪行。

——丘吉尔

2010 年 7 月，北大前任校长许智宏去深圳，点名约见两位在"各行各业都做得很出色"的北大校友。

其中一位就是"卖猪肉"的北大校友，广东天地集团的总裁陈生。

陈生，广东湛江人，北京大学经济学学士，清华 EMBA。1984 年北大毕业后被分配在广州一个机关单位，每天过着重复，枯燥，没滋没味的日子，还得忍受单位里论资排辈，尔虞我诈的郁闷氛围。他觉得再这样混下去，简直就是浪费生命。

三年后，他选择辞去"铁饭碗"，"下海"了。

20 世纪 80 年代，自己砸掉人人羡慕的机关"铁饭碗"，那得需要多大勇气！

"下海"之后，他倒腾过服装，倒腾过白酒，也倒腾过房地产。而且倒腾房地产还倒腾出了不小的动静，但他最终还是选择了"卖猪肉"。2006 年，他打造自己的土猪养殖场，2007 年开始在广州开猪肉档卖猪

My Love for My Duty

You can't do what you love, you should love
what you do.

——Winston Churchill

In July 2010, former president of Peking University Xu Zhihong went to Shenzhen to meet two alumnus of Peking University in particular, who were representatives of "excelling in all walks of life".

One of them is Chen Sheng, Peking University's graduate that "sells pork" and he's also a president of Guangdong Tiandi Group.

Chen Sheng, born in Zhanjiang, Guangdong Province, is the bachelor of economics of Peking University and EMBA of Tsinghua University. In 1984, he was distributed to a government unit in Guangzhou where he lived same boring life every day and had to withstand the system of superiority according to seniority in an aggressive environment. He thought it was totally a waste of life if he continued to work here.

Three years later, he chose to give up the secure job and start his own business.

How brave he was to refuse the enviable "iron bowl" working in a government organ in 1980s.

After he resigned, he sold clothes, liquor and worked in the real estate And he did well real estate. But he eventually chose to sell pork. In 2006, he built his own organic pig farm and sold pork in Guangzhou in 2007.

131

肉，短短两年时间在广州开设近100家"壹号土猪"连锁店，营业额达到2亿元，被人称为广州的"猪肉大王"。

有人问他："房地产赚钱又快又轻松，为什么还要卖肉呢？"

他说："房地产赚钱轻松且快不假，但不符合我的性格，我还是安安分分养好我的猪吧。与其天天陪人喝酒赔笑脸，我更愿意跟阳光打交道。"

陈生说，当然，北大校友卖猪肉也要卖出"北大水平"来。2005年的一天，陈生去农贸市场逛看别人卖猪肉，这一看让他大吃一惊。农贸市场里那么多卖猪肉的，但没有一个猪肉有品牌，有形象。回来后他就着手调查猪肉市场数据，他发现全国6.5亿头猪，以一头猪100斤算就可卖1000元，全国猪肉市场一年就有1万亿元的销售额。几乎没有一个行业能有如此大的市场容量！

他越研究越有兴趣，他觉得如果他去卖电脑，他得面临像联想等这些有着几百亿上千亿资产的企业竞争，但是卖猪肉，他是北大经济系毕业的高才生，与竞争对手相比，他有与众不同的经济头脑。他决心要在这个行业里干一点"伟大"的事，人家一天卖一头猪、半头猪，他就要卖几十头，几百头，这就是"北大水平"。

如今的陈生，经常待在广州郊区的一个农庄里忙活着他的猪肉事业，也在那里办公。在阳光、清风与憨拙的土猪陪伴下，自得其乐地工作。

可是，现实生活中，我们有多少人能够"自得其乐"地做自己喜欢的工作呢？

股神巴菲特说："做自己喜欢的事，还能有钱赚，这是件最快乐的事。"巴菲特被邀至哥伦比亚大学演讲，当被问到他成功的秘诀时，巴菲特开怀大笑起来，他说与在座的学生们相比，他并无不同之处，如果

Within just two years, he opened almost 100 chain stores of "No.1 Organic Pork" in Guangzhou with sales revenue reaching 200 million yuan, earning himself a name "King of Pork".

Someone asked him, "it is easy to make money in real estate, why do you sell pork?"

He said, "it is true that real estate is profitable and easy, but it is not suitable for me. I prefer to raise my pigs. I would rather live under the sun than drink and fake smile with others for business."

Chen Sheng said, of course, even selling pork, graduated from Peking Universitiy can also exhibit the best performance of the University. One day in 2005, he was surprised when he went to the market of agricultural produce and saw others selling pork. There were so many merchants selling pork in the market, but there was no brand of the pork. When he returned, he began to search market data and found that there were 650 million pigs nationwide. If a pig weighted 100 catties can be sold at 1,000 yuan, the total sales volume of the national pork market would reach 1 trillion yuan. There is no other industries that can be compared to the pork market.

The more he researched into the field, the more he became interested. He thought, "if he sells computers, he has to compete with companies worth over tens of billions or even hundreds of billions yuan like Lenovo. But if he sells pork, as a graduate of economics of Peking University, he has a different business mind when compared with competitors. He was determined to start a great business. When others sell a pig or half a pig a day, he should sell tens or hundreds, which is the performance of Peking University.

Today, Chen Sheng often stays in a farm on the outskirts of Guangzhou, busy with his pork career and also does his business there. With the companion of sunlight, breeze and simple clumsy pigs, he works with great happiness.

However, in real life, how many of us can work with happiness by doing our favourite work?

Warren Buffett said, "the greatest happiness is to do your favorite things while you are making money." When Buffett delivered a speech at the invitation of the Columbia University and asked about the secret of his

一定要说有的话，那就是他每天都在做自己最喜欢的工作。

"每天都在做自己最喜欢的工作。"这短短几个字，其实是大多数人穷其一生都无法实现的美丽梦想。

绝大多数人的现状是，清晨勉强睁开困乏的眼睛，不情不愿地挤着车去上班，熬到太阳落山，心力交瘁腰酸背痛地下班。厌倦、烦躁、倦怠常常袭击我们早已脆弱的心。有久未联系的朋友打来电话："最近过得怎么样？""唉，老样子，没劲。"

有个故事里说一个观光团去一个山水秀美的偏僻小村去游玩，一个当地老人坐在树荫下一边吹着凉风一边编草帽，那草帽是用当地的一种蒲草编的，非常精致漂亮。观光团里的一个商人看见了欣喜若狂，他想，这样漂亮精美的草帽，如果拿到大城市去卖，价钱一定不菲。

商人压住内心的狂喜，装作不经意地问老人："请问，这草帽多少钱一顶啊？"老人微笑着说："十块钱。"说完又低头继续编他的草帽了，老人边编草帽边哼着小调儿，看上去快乐而闲适。

商人高兴得快跳起来，这么精致的帽子在大城市，没有一百块是绝对买不到的。商人赶紧对老人说："老人家，如果我在您这里订做一万顶草帽的话，你每顶能给我优惠多少钱呢？"

他以为老人肯定会高兴坏了，没想到老人慢吞吞地说："要是这样的话，我就不卖给你了。"商人大惑不解。老人说："我坐在这树荫底下编草帽，吹着风，喝着茶，哼着歌，本来是很享受的事，没有一点负担。你要一万顶帽子，我就得没日没夜地拼命干，那该多累啊，不但身体累，我的心更累呢，所以我不愿卖了。"

当工作不是一种享受，而成为一种心灵的负累时，我们就会有疲惫不堪、心力交瘁的感觉。

success, he laughed, saying that there was no difference between him and the students at present, and if there had to be something different, it was that he could do his favorite job every day.

"Do your favorite work every day." This sentence has a few words, but in fact, it is a beautiful dream that many people can never realize throughout their life.

The status quo of the vast majority is to strive to open their eyes in the morning and go to work on crowded commutes with reluctance, and get home with pains and fatigue. Boredom, irritability, and burnout often attack our already fragile heart. A friend who has not been contacted for a long time called, "How's your life?" "Alas, same as before it's boring."

There is a story about a trip to a beautiful remote village of a tourist group. An old local man was sitting in the shade with blowing cool breeze while weaving straw hat. The straw hat was made of a local plant, very delicate and beautiful. A businessman of the tourist group was so ecstatic, as he thought, it must earn a lot of money to sell such beautiful and delicate hats in big cities.

With holding his excitement inside, the businessman pretended to ask the old man unintentionally, "Excuse me, how much is this straw hat?" The old man smily answered, "Ten yuan." And then continued to weave the hat. He seemed so happy and carefree, weaving the hat while humming a wandering tune.

The businessman was so excited that he even jumped up. It is impossible to buy such a delicate hat with less than 100 yuan in big cities. He told the old man immediately, "Should there be any discount if I order 10,000 hats from you."

The businessman thought the old man would be very happy to hear about this. To his great surprise, the old man responded slowly, "If so, I will not sell you any hat." The businessman was perplexed. The old man said, "Sitting under the tree while weaving a straw hat, feeling the breeze, drinking the tea and humming a song, how enjoyable it is without any pressure. But if you want 10, 000 hats, I will need to meet your demand working day and night. How tiresome it is, not only for my body but also for my heart. So, I will not sell it."

易中天给女儿选专业时的建议是：第一考虑兴趣，第二考虑自己的优势，第三考虑创造性，第四考虑将来是否挣钱。

当然，也许有些人会对易中天的建议不认同，因为我们往往会迫于生活的压力，不得不从事一份自己不喜欢的工作。先要生存，然后才有可能去追求更多的东西。

既然目前不得不做我们不喜欢的这份工作，与其成天念叨"我不喜欢这工作，我好累……"让自己如行尸走肉一样活着，不如调整自己，把目前从事的工作当成必要的过渡与磨炼，让它成为通向你喜欢的那份工作的桥梁。

终有一天，你会惊喜地发现你已达到罗素所说的人生目标——"我之所爱为我天职"。

载于《意林》

智慧箴言

好多时候，我们都会碰到这样的问题：你最想做什么？每个人都知道自己想干什么，可是没多少人能坚持去干自己想干的。你知道自己想干什么吗？你有勇气坚持吗？

When work is not an enjoyment but a burden of the soul, we will feel exhausted and tired.

When Yi Zhongtian's daughter chose her major, the recommended considerations given by him is: the first, interest; the second, advantage; the third, creativity and finally, profitability.

Of course, some people may not agree with Yi Zhongtian's proposal, because we are often forced by the pressure of life, we have to engage in a job we do not like. The first thing is to survive and then it is possible to pursue more.

Now that we have to do this job we do not like, rather than talk about all day that "I do not like this work, I'm tired..." to allow ourselves living like a zombie every day, it is better to adjust ourselves to the current work as the necessary transition and make it a bridge to your favorite job.

Eventually, you will be surprised to find that you have reached the life goal described by Russell, "My love is my duty".

We will often encounter such a problem: what do you want to do most? Everyone knows what they want, but not many people insist on doing what they want. Do you know what you want to do? Do you have the courage to insist on?

梦想从来不卑微

文 / 李红都

世上最快乐的事，不过是为梦想奋斗。

——苏格拉底

他的噩梦是从三岁那年开始的。

那天，母亲终于从亲友们"贵人行迟"的安慰声中省悟过来，抱着浑身瘫软的他坐上火车直奔省城的儿科医院。大夫无情的诊断打碎了母亲最后一丝希望，"重度脑瘫，像这种情况目前尚无康复的前例"。母亲抱着他，哭了个天昏地暗。丈夫说："把他送到福利院吧，我们再生一个。"她不依，为此丈夫和她翻了脸，一纸离婚证，从此他与她成了陌路。

为了照顾他的生活，并有足够时间带他看病，母亲辞去了工作，带他住进了福利院。好心的院长在福利院后勤部给她安排了一份洗衣做饭的工作，让她得以边工作边照顾他。

八岁那年，他终于站了起来，但他的四肢并不听从大脑的指挥：他的十指痉挛地扭曲着不能合拢，腿也笨拙得迈不出直线，用"张牙舞爪"来形容他走路的样子，倒真有些生动形象……

Dream is Never Humble

The happiest thing in life is to struggle for dreams.

—— Socrates

His nightmare began from the age of three.

On that day, as soon as the mother finally realized the truth from the comfort of his relatives and friends that "the noble often moves late than others", she took him, who was too soft to move, on the train towards the provincial pediatric hospital. The doctor's ruthless diagnosis broke the last hope of his mother, "Severe cerebral palsy, which has no cases of rehabilitation until now". Holding him in her arms, his mother cried heartbrokenly. Her husband said, "How about sending him to the welfare house and we can give birth to a another baby." She refused. As a result, her husband turned against her and divorced with her, became a stranger in her life.

In order to take care of him, and have enough time to take him to see a doctor, his mother resigned her job and moved to live in the welfare with him. Kind-hearted dean of the welfare offered her a job of cooking and laundry in the logistics department so that she could work while taking care of him.

He finally stood up when he was 8, but his limbs did not listen to the command of the brain: his fingers were twisting and could not draw close to each other and his legs were too clumsy to walk in straight line. It was quite vivid to describe the way he walked with "baring his fangs and opening his claws".

139

虽然走路的样子不雅观，但他总算能独自站立行走了。母亲多少感到一丝欣慰。只是，他的情况太特殊，尽管早已过了上学的年龄，却没有一家学校愿意接收他。

　　母亲找来别的小孩子用过的小学课本，用有限的文化教他学习拼音和汉字。他歪着脸口齿不清地叫她："老——师——"她看着他明亮的眼眸笑成了一朵花，转过身却飞速地用手背擦去眼角溢出来的泪花。

　　十八岁那年，县残联推荐他和另外几位重度残疾人参加市残联举办的残疾人职业技能培训班。首次接触电脑的他，一下子被电脑中变幻莫测又精美异常的图案迷住了。

　　他决心攻下软件知识，便报名参加了电脑初级班的学习。教室里，辅导他的老师甚至有些不忍心看他，因为他的双手严重扭曲，每在电脑上敲打一个字，全身都要跟着一起使劲。尝试了多次，他依然不能像常人一样将十指准确地放在键盘上完成盲打的训练，他只好用两个大拇指轮流着击打键盘，艰难地完成了打字的训练。

　　电脑班结业后，他开始想办法用有限的电脑知识找工作，但是，面对他这样一个路都走不稳，手指也不灵活的重残者，根本就没有单位敢接收。看着镜子里的自己唇上已长出细密的"绒毛"，却仍靠头发花白的母亲在福利院给人洗衣做饭赚到的几百元工资生存，他恨自己没用。

　　他想死，母亲说："我现在除了你，什么也没有了，你要是死了，我也不想活了。"他拉着母亲的手，号啕大哭。

　　哭过后，他做出了一个决定："既然没人要我，我就自个儿给自个儿打工。"

　　母亲吓了一跳，摸了摸他的头，不是发烧了吧？他忍着泪，拼命调整好不听话的表情肌，给了母亲一个微笑……

Though he could not walk elegantly, after all he could stand up and walk on his own. His mother was gratified. However, his case was too special. Though he was already over the age for schooling, no school was willing to accept him.

His mother used the primary school textbooks of other children to teach him to learn Pinyin and Chinese characters with her limited education. Tilting his head, he called her with a twist in his tongue, "tea—cher—". Staring at his bright eyes, there was a flower in her eyes, and turned around to quickly wipe the tears burst out from her eyes with the back of her hand.

When he was 18 years old, he, together with other severely disabled people, was recommended to participate in vocational skills training courses held by municipal federation of the disabled people. He was suddenly enchanted by the unpredictable and unusually beautiful pictures in the computer the first time he touched it.

He was determined to master software knowledge and was enrolled in the primary computer courses. In the classroom, the teacher could not bear to look at him, as his hands are seriously distorted. His body must follow hard together even he tried to type a single word. Trying again and again, he still failed to complete the practice of blind typing very accurately with all his fingers on the keyboard like an ordinary man. Therefore, he had to use two thumbs to hit the keyboard in turn, and complete the typing training in difficulties.

After graduating from the computer course, he tried to find a job with his limited computer knowledge. But no firm dared to accept a man with severe disabilities like him who could not even walk steadily, let alone his inflexible fingers. Looking at the man in the mirror with peach-fuzz beard on his lip who depended on his gray-haired mother who still did laundry and cooking in the welfare house to earn several hundred yuan a month, he hated his uselessness.

He wanted to die, but his mother said, "I have nothing but you now. If you die, I don't want to live." He took his mother's hands, howling loudly.

After crying, he made a decision, "Since no one wants me, I will be my own boss."

Shocked, his mother touched his head to see if he had a fever. He held

捧起一位好心人送的《photoshop CS教材》，他在别人淘汰下来的电脑上一点点地摸索。

　　一年后，他已能用"二指禅"熟练地在电脑上设计各类平面广告。他对设计近乎痴迷的热爱打动了每一位认识他的人，母亲也动心了——也许行动不便的他真的适合走这条路呢。

　　在母亲拼尽全力的努力和社会上几位爱心人士的帮助下，一家小小的广告公司成立了，他是老板，也是员工。不懂电脑的母亲，是他的业务联系人，同时也是他的保姆，照顾他的生活起居。在这间用租来的民房改造成的小公司中，临街的那间"门面房"就是他的"经理办公室"，里面的一间是他和母亲的卧室兼厨房。

　　身体的残障加上他与社会接触面的局限，生意很冷清，常来光临的客户多是周围了解并同情他们母子生活的居民。

　　空闲时候，他最喜欢的事便是和母亲一起憧憬未来：他的业务在不断发展；一位心地善良的好姑娘在人生路上成为他的伴侣，辅助他成就更大的事业，买下一套不大也不小的房子容纳他们纯美的爱情；母亲终于苦尽甘来，穿着漂亮时尚的衣裳，戴着珠宝项链，想去哪儿就去哪儿，想买什么都买得起。

　　母亲疼爱地看着他，笑而不语。曾经，她以为他能走路、能自己吃饭、能依靠她微薄的薪水生存下去，她便很欣慰。不承想，他居然能用这么严重的残疾之躯，走上自强自立的路。在母亲心中，无论他是怎样的残疾，他都是她心里最棒的孩子。

　　两年后，他的业务水平日渐完善，但生意仍然时好时差，收入仅够维持朴素的日常生活。妻子和房子，对目前的他来说，仍是个遥远的梦想。

　　在这个流光溢彩的城市中，他们无疑是挣扎在社会底层的小人物，

back the tears, desperately adjusting the expression of the disobedient muscle to smile to his mother.

With a *Instruction on Photoshop CS* brought by a kind man, he learnt little by little on an old computer discarded by someone else.

One year later, he could proficiently design different print ads on computer only with his two thumbs. His obsession with design touches all the people who know him. Even his mother is touched—maybe this is a suitable path for him who has difficulties in movement.

With his mother's great efforts and support from several kinds people in society, a small advertising firm was set up. He was the boss and the employee. His mother, who knew nothing about computer, helped him contact customers and served as his nurse to take care of his life. In this small company established in the rented residential house, the room along the street was his "General Manager's Office" and another room inside was the bedroom for his mother and him and the kitchen.

Physical disability has limited his social contact. The business was not good and clients were primarily those nearby residents sympathetic for them.

When he was free, he loved to envsion the future with his mother: his business is developing; a kind girl becomes his wife and helps him to enlarge his business. He can afford a house of modest size to accommodate their pure love; his mother finally has the chance to enjoy her life, wearing beautiful clothes and jewelry necklaces, and can go everywhere she wants and affords everything she likes.

His mother looked at him lovingly, smiling without words. Once, she thought she would be consoled if he could walk, eat on his own, and live on her meager salary. She had never expected that he could embark on a road of self-reliance with such a severely disabled body. In his mother's mind, no matter how disabled he is, he is the best child in her heart.

Two years later, his business is gradually turning well but is still unstable. He can just sustain a simple life. For him, wife and house are still distant dreams.

In this colorful city, they are actually nameless figures striving at the

重度的身体残障更是给他的生活刻上了卑微的烙印。但是，他的梦想却从来都不曾卑微。

或许，他的梦想只能停留在幻想的美好世界中，但那又有什么关系？因为正是那些可能一生也实现不了的梦想，才让他有了拼搏的力量，带着回报母爱的心愿，一步一步艰难却执着地行走在人生的道路上。

载于《意林·原创版》

智慧箴言

人的一生该有两样东西值得仰望：头顶灿烂的星空和心中坚定的信仰。无论路有多远，机会有多迷茫，在值得坚持的时候都不要把时间只用来低落了，去相信，去孤单，去爱去恨去浪费，去闯去梦去后悔。没有人可以拯救你，就像没有人能够打败你一样！

bottom of the society. Severe physical disability has engraved a humble branding. But his dreams are never humble.

Maybe, his dream can only exist in fantasy, but does that matter? It is the dream that cannot be realized that offers them strength to struggle. A wish to repay his mother's love that enables him to march on his life road even in face of difficulties.

There are two things worth respect in a man's life: the starry night overhead and a determined mind. No matter how far the road is, how confused the opportunity is, it is unnecessary to feel depressed. Take time to believe, even alone, to love and hate, to waste, to struggle, to dream and regret. Nobody can save you just as no one can defeat you!

稻草与大树

文 / 李兴海

> 信念是鸟，它在黎明仍然黑暗之际，感觉到了光
> 明，唱出了歌。
>
> ——泰戈尔

我与你一样，时刻在想，如何向后一辈的人阐述信念的重要性，以及信念为何物。当我在公共场合有意传达这类思想时，旁人经常会讪讪地问我："信念能吃吗？能填饱肚子吗？"

信念如梦想一般，纯属虚无之物，飘渺至极。没人能说出信念的形貌，体态，或者是年龄。它与我们不仅仅是天涯之隔，甚至可以说，它从始至终就没有在人类历史的长河中显现过。

那么，我何以要推崇并且宣扬它呢？原因很简单，它对所有存活于世间的生物都有着不可言喻的功用。

很多人问过我，有什么功用？难不成能把所有的人都变成比尔·盖茨，变成爱因斯坦？当然不能，信念本身需要生命作为载体，而每一个生命所具有的天性都存有细微的差别。因此，注定会创造不同的历史，取得不同的成就。

Straw and Big Trees

Faith is a bird, who feels light and sings songs even when the dawn is still dark.

——Tagore

Like you, I am always thinking about how to explain the importance of beliefs and what beliefs are to backward people. When I intended to convey the idea in public, people often asked me ,awkward: "can you eat faith? Can you fill your belly with it?"

Faith, like dreams, is nothing but a very ethereal thing. No one can tell the appearance, the posture, or the age of a belief. It is not only the distance between heaven and earth with us, and even can be said that it never appeared in the history of the human being.

So why should I praise and advertise it? The reason is very simple, it has a ineffable function to all living creatures in the world.

A lot of people have asked me, "What's the function? Is it possible to turn all the people into Bill Gates or Einstein?" Of course not, belief itself requires life as a carrier, and each life has a subtle difference in its nature. Therefore, it is destined to create different history and achieve different achievements.

很久以前，我曾教过一个调皮，又极具文学天赋的孩子。我每日闲暇时必会催促他，专心攻于写作。可他不爱遵从我的吩咐，他说，文字是在心中，并非跃于纸上。可我知道，他仅仅只是懒于动身提笔。

　　他和很多人一样，而这类人什么年龄段的都有。自己本身心存希冀，尚有鸿鹄大志，却不甘脚踏实地，为此志就地挥汗。于是，时日一长，所见收效甚微，胸中大志便成了小志，最后，全然无志。无志不说，还好提"当年勇"。

　　大怒之时，我曾骂过他，心中毫无半点信念。他如旁人一般问我："何为信念？你能指给我看吗？"

　　我领着他，穿过城市的车水马龙，来到秋日的田野上。

　　弯腰割稻的辛勤劳动者与金黄的果实构成了一幅绝美的画面。我步入田野之中，随手拣起一根稻草，放到他的手里，让他开怀抱住这根稻草，并做一个双脚离地的动作给我看。

　　他见我异常严肃，便一声不吭地抱住那根如筷子般粗细的稻草，试图双脚离地。可这样的事，终究是不会成功的。最后，他一脸委屈地说："我做不到。"

　　路旁，一棵茂盛的大树正迎风招展。我指着壮实的树干对他说："你抱着它，并做一个双脚离地的动作给我看。"

　　他欣喜地双手抱树，一跃而起，双脚离地蹬于树干之上，"噌噌"几下爬了上去。然后站在高高的树枝上冲着我笑，像是在炫耀他的技艺。

　　我问他："上面的景色美吗？"他对着一望无垠的田野远眺几次后大声地告诉我，美！美极了！

　　我令他下树之后，拍拍他的肩膀道："你刚才所抱的两种东西，就是我平日所说的信念。"他不解地看着我。

　　"信念虽是虚无之物，可你却能拥抱，或是依靠着它来行路。只有

A long time ago, I used to teach an naughty and gifted literary child. My daily spare time would urge him to concentrate on writing. But he did not like to follow my instructions, he said, "words are in his heart, not on paper." I know that he is just too lazy to write.

He's like many people else, and this kind of people are of every age. Their hope is ambitious, but unwilling to sweat in this work. So, after a long time, they did little, ambitions became small, finally, no ambition. No ambition is fine, but also to mention "previous deeds."

When I was furious, I scolded him that he had no faith in heart. He asked me, as someone else, "What is faith? Can you show me?"

I took him through the heavy traffic of the city, and arrive at autumn fields.

Bent over the rice, the hard-working workers and the golden fruits make a beautiful picture. I stepped into the field, picked up a straw and put it in his hand. I asked him to embrace the straw and show me the action of moving his feet off the ground.

He found that I was very seriously, so he silently hugged straw as thick as a chopstick, trying to got his feet off the ground. But such a thing will never succeed. Finally, he said with an aggrieved face, "I can't do it."

A lush tree is fluttering in the wind on the roadside. I pointed to the sturdy trunk and said to him, "you hold it, do a double foot off the ground".

He was delighted to hold the tree with hands, sprang up, feet off the ground. Quickly climbed up the tree trunk. Then he stood on the high branch of the tree, smiling at me, as if to show off his skills.

I asked him, "Is the scenery above beautiful?" He was overlooking the boundless field several times and loudly told me that it was beauty! Very beautiful!

When I asked him walk down the tree, I patted him on the shoulder and said, "The two things you've just held are beliefs what I usually say." He looked at me puzzled.

当某一日你心生绝望，或是豁然开朗时你才会明白，它就在你身旁。也许，它是刚才那根弱不禁风的稻草，任凭你如何努力，也无法与困境脱离。也许，它就是面前的这棵大树，既能让你无畏风雨，又能让你站得更高。"

刚说完这些话，田野上就起了秋风。那些杂乱的稻草再次被席卷得狼狈不堪。不远处，一棵大树正立于狂风中，"哗哗"地朝空中咆哮。

载于《中学生》

智 慧 箴 言

> 信念是黑暗中的光亮，信念让我们在极度痛苦中找到自我。
> 无论在多么艰难，多么困苦的环境中，只要我们拥有坚定的信念，我们就可以迎难而上。

"Although faith can't be seen, you can embrace or rely on it for your journey. It is only when you become desperate or suddenly enlightened that you can realize that it is beside you. Perhaps, it is just the weak straw, no matter how hard you are, you can not get out of dilemma. Maybe it is a big tree like this one, which can make you fearless and help you stand taller."

As soon as these words were finished, the autumn wind rose from the fields. The jumble of straw was again swept the crumpled. Not far away, a big tree standing in the wind, roar into the air.

Faith is the light in the darkness. Faith allows us to find ourselves in great pain.

No matter how the environment is, we can go forward with solid belief.

靠自己

文 / 温美

我愿靠自己的力量打开我的前途，而不愿求有力者的垂青。

——雨果

有一天，大仲马得知自己的儿子小仲马寄出的稿子接连碰壁，便对小仲马说："如果你能在寄稿时，随稿给编辑先生们附上一封短信，或者只是一句话，说'我是大仲马的儿子'，或许情况就会好多了。"

小仲马倔强地说："不，我不想坐在你的肩头上摘苹果，那样摘来的苹果没味道。"年轻的小仲马不但拒绝以父亲的盛名做自己事业的敲门砖，而且不露声色地给自己取了十几个其他姓氏的笔名，以避免那些编辑先生们把他和大名鼎鼎的父亲联系起来。

面对那些冷酷无情的一张张退稿笺，小仲马没有沮丧，仍在屡败屡战地坚持创作自己的作品。

他的长篇小说《茶花女》寄出后，终于以其绝妙的构思和精彩的文笔震撼了一位资深望重的编辑。这位编辑曾和大仲马有着多年的书信来往，他看到寄稿人的地址同大仲马的地址丝毫不差，怀疑是大仲马另取

Depend on Yourself

I prefer to rely on own strength to open my future, not for image.

——Hugo

One day, Alexandre Dumas knew that works sent out by his son Alexandre Dumas Fils were rejected, therefore he told his son, "If you can attach a letter to editors or just a sentence that 'I am the son of Alexandre Dumas' to your manuscript, perhaps the situation will be much better."

Dumas stubbornly said, "No, I do not want to sit on your shoulder to pick apples, as those apples are tasteless." Young Alexnadre Dumas Fils not only refused to use his father's fame as a stepping stone for his career, but also quietly made several last names as his pseudonym so as to avoid being linked with his outstanding father by those editors.

Facing those ruthless rejection letters, he was not frustrated. Instead, he insisted on creating his own work despite continual rejections.

When his novel *La Traviata* was sent, its wonderful idea and excellent writing shocked a senior editor. The editor had many years of correspondence with Alexandre Dumas. He saw the sender's address was the same as Alexandre Dumas', thus suspecting that if this was Dumas' another pen name, but the style of the works was very different from that of

的笔名，但作品的风格却和大仲马的迥然不同。这位编辑带着兴奋和疑问，迫不及待地乘车造访大仲马家。

令他大吃一惊的是，《茶花女》这部伟大的作品，作者竟是名不见经传的大仲马的儿子小仲马。

"您为何不在稿子上署上您的真实姓名呢？"这位编辑疑惑地问小仲马。

小仲马说："我只想拥有真实的高度。"

这位编辑对小仲马的做法赞叹不已。

《茶花女》出版后，法国文坛的评论家一致认为，这部作品的价值远远超过了大仲马的代表作《基督山伯爵》。小仲马靠自己的力量攀登到文坛的高峰。

美国物理学家富兰克林，是家中十二个男孩中最小的。由于家境贫寒，他十二岁就到哥哥开的小印刷所去当学徒。他把排字当作学习写作的好机会，从不叫苦。

不久，富兰克林认识了几个在书店当学徒的小伙伴，经常通过他们借书看。随着阅读数量的增加，他逐渐能学着写些小文章了。

在富兰克林十五岁时，他哥哥筹办了一份报纸《新英格兰新闻》。报上常登载一些文学小品，很受读者的欢迎。

富兰克林也想试一试文笔，但又不想通过哥哥来登载自己的文章。为此，富兰克林化名写了一篇小文章，趁半夜没人时把稿子悄悄地放在印刷所的门口。

第二天一早，他哥哥看到那篇稿件，便请来一些经常写作的朋友审阅评论。那些人一致称赞是篇好文章，有一位诗人竟断定，这是出自名家的手笔。

从此，富兰克林的文章经常在报上发表，但他的哥哥一直不知道

Dumas. Therefore, the editor with excitement and doubt, could not wait to travel to visit Dumas.

To his surprise, the great work *La Traviata* was created by Dumas' son, an unknown author Alexandre Dumas Fils.

"Why don't you write your real name on the manuscript?" Confused, the editor asked Dumas Fils.

He said, "I just want to reach where I should be."

The editor greatly praised him.

When *La Traviata* was published, all the French literary critics agreed that the value of this work was far more than the Dumas' masterpiece *Enchantment of Monte Cristo*. Dumas Fils climbed to the peak of the literary world with his own strength.

Franklin, the American physicist, was the youngest of 12 boys in the family. Due to his poor family, he worked as an apprentice in his brother's small printing shop when 12 years old. He treated typography as a good opportunity to learn to write, never complaining about it.

Shortly after, he made friends with several apprentices working in local book stores so that he could borrow books from them. Growing reading enabled him to learn to write some small articles gradually.

When he was 15, his brother set up *New England News* in which some literature works were published and widely welcomed.

Franklin wanted to try writing as well. But he did not want to make his articles accepted as a result of his brother. Therefore, he used a fake name to write an article and put it quietly in front of the door of the printing shop during midnight.

The next morning when his brother saw the article, he invited some friends who regularly wrote to review and offer comments. The article got unanimous praise. One poet even suggested it must be wrote by a famous writer.

From then on, his articles were usually published in the newspaper, but his brother had no idea who the author was. Afterwards, his brother decided to find it out by hiding at the door of the printing shop in midnight.

真正的作者是谁。后来，他哥哥决心要破解这个谜，在半夜时藏在印刷所门口，但他做梦也没想到这位"名家"竟是自己的弟弟小富兰克林。

……

毋庸讳言，以人取言，人微言轻，近水楼台先得月，老子英雄儿好汉等不公平的现象，目前还是比较常见的，就是在将来也是难以完全避免的。但是，与其怨天尤人哀叹自己的命运，倒不如脚踏实地增强自己的实力。从长远的观点看问题，任何事物发展的根本原因，不在事物的外部，而在事物的内部。外因是变化的条件，内因是变化的根据。在这个意义上可以说，人人都是自己命运的设计师，最可依靠的不是任何人的权力和威望，而是自己的力量。

"滴自己的汗，吃自己的饭；自己的事，自己干；靠人靠天靠祖上，不算是好汉。"郑板桥的这些话，当然不是主张可以忽视前进中可以借用的力量，而是强调千靠万靠，不如自靠的主张。

载于《语文报》

智 慧 箴 言

　　不管我们踩什么样的高跷，没有自己的脚是不行的。淌自己的汗，吃自己的饭，自己的事情自己干，靠天靠地靠祖上，不算是好汉。通往幸福的钥匙靠自己开启，每个人书写人生的笔，都握在自己的手里。

Never had he thought that this "famous" author was his younger brother Franklin.

…

Needless to say, unjust phenomena such as value remarks based on the speaker and nameless figure's remarks are always unimportant, a person in a favorable position gains special advantages, and the son of a hero is also a brave man, are still common at present and cannot be totally avoided even in the future. But, instead of complaining about destiny, it is better to make concerted efforts. From a long-term perspective, the fundamental reason for the development of things rests not on the external environment but on the internal situation. External factor is the condition of changes while the internal factor is the basis of changes. In light of this, people are designers of their own destiny and what they can rely on is not the power or fame of others but their own strength.

"Mind your own business and do your work on your own. It is not a true man to rely on others, God or ancestors." Instead of ignoring the sources that can be used to move forwards, these remarks of Zheng Banqiao propose the importance of relying on yourself instead of others.

No matter what kind of stilts we step on, it is impossible to walk without our own feet. Do you own work and it is not a true man to rely on others God or ancestors. The key to happiness is in your own hands and the pen to write your own life is in your hand.

第三辑 抬起我们的头

Series 3　Raise Our Heads

　　当你只是一个烹饪师时，你烹制出了许多美味，也就抓住了民众之根本，同时也抓住了自己的人生之根本。如果你有幸被民众推举成为"治大国"的官员，倘或依然去"烹小鲜"，且忙得不亦乐乎，而忘了"治大国"的责任，也就丢了人生之根本。有些事，尽管它成全了你，也可以将它忘一忘，如此才能适应新的身份，能在新的岗位上做出更好的业绩，满足人们对你新的期盼。

　　When you are a cook, you can make many delicious dishes and secure the fundamental need of the public and the essence of your life. When you are lucky to be elected as an important governor to deal with state affairs, but if you are still busy in cooking and forget your responsibility, you will lose the essence of life. A certain thing may make who you are, you should still set it aside to adapt to a new identity so that you can fulfill your commitment and satisfy the new expectations of you.

不要仅仅活在当下

文/［美］萨妮·戈德 孙开元 编译

兼听则明，偏信则暗。

——《新唐书·魏征传》

人们在长期的社会生活中总结了很多生活经验，这些经验让我们受益匪浅，少走了许多弯路。但是如今一些研究者发现，人们很多习以为常的经验并非放之四海而皆准，比如下面这些。

1. 直视对方，更有说服力

我们早就听说：直视对方的眼睛，能表达出你的真诚。但是如果你想劝说朋友做某件事，比如探险旅行，最好不要直视对方为妙。在最近一项研究中，研究者使用目光追踪技术发现，说话时目光注视对方时间最长的人，能说服对方的可能性反而较小，除非是对方早已经认可了说话者的观点。"目光接触能够传递出大不相同的信息，可以是喜欢或感兴趣，也可以是挑战或恐吓。"此次研究的领导人、英国哥伦比亚大学心理学助理教授弗朗西斯·奇恩说。要想预见对方的反应，要考虑听者的身份和你言语中的要旨。在一个友好的氛围中，目光接触能够使双方

Do Not Just Live in the Moment

Listen to both side and you will be enlightened.

——New Book of Tang Biography of Weizheng

People accumulate a lot of life experience in long-term social life, which brings considerable benefits and avoids many detours for us. But now some researchers have found that much of the experience that people have become accustomed to is not universally applicable, such as the following.

1. It is more convincing to look directly at each other

We have long heard of that looking at someone's eyes can express your sincerity. But if you want to persuade a friend to do something, such as an adventure, it is better not to look at your object. In a recent study, researchers, using eye-tracking techniques, have found that the person who gazes at the other person for the longest time is less likely to persuade the other person unless he/she has already agree with the speaker's point of view. "Eye contact can convey very different information. It can means attraction or interest and can also be challenge or intimidation." Said by Francis Kian, the study leader and assistant professor of psychology at Columbia University. To anticipate the other people's reactions, it is necessary to consider the identity of the listener and the purpose of your speech. However, if in a friendly atmosphere, eye contact can enhance the

增进了解。而在一个互相敌视的氛围中，直视对方可能具有挑战意味。

2. 拍照增强记忆

拿着相机拍下照片，把记忆保留下来，这听起来好像无可厚非，但是美国康涅狄州费尔菲尔德大学的一项新研究发现，拍照不但会在当时阻碍你尽情享受本应体验到的快乐，还会在以后削弱你回忆时的印象。在这次研究中，研究者让多位受试者在博物馆里尽可能详细地记下一些指定的物品，拍照或者只是观看，两种方法任选其一。第二天，拍照的那些位受试者中较少有人能叫出所拍物品的名称，也较少能记住那些物品的细节。费尔菲尔德大学心理学教授琳达·汉克尔说："原因可能是这样的：在按下快门的那一刻，我们就暗示自己'完事大吉，该做下一件事了……'，于是大脑就不会再做出可以增强记忆的一些活动。"

3. 多说"我"，显自信

你也许觉得经常把"我"字挂在嘴边的人都很自信，但是得克萨斯大学的一些研究者最近做了一项研究，他们对人们的对话和电子邮件进行分类，发现那些频繁地使用"我"的人，比那些使用这个词频率较低的人更缺少自信。"（我、你、他）之类的代词反映了我们的注意力关注在哪里。"研究者之一、得克萨斯大学心理学教授詹姆斯·彭尼贝克说。喜欢使用"我"的人关注自身，可能是因为自我意识强、有不安全感，或者迫切地想得到他人的喜欢。相反，那些自信的人使用频率更多的词是"你"，他们把大部分注意力投向了外部世界，并且希望得到积极的反馈信息。

understanding of both sides. In a hostile atmosphere, it may be challenging to look directly at the other one.

2. Take pictures to strengthen memories

It is acceptable to take pictures to keep memories. But a new study of the University of Fairfield in Connecticut found that taking pictures will not only prevent you from enjoying the pleasure you should have experienced at that time, but also weaken your impression of memories in retrospect. In this study, the researcher asked multiple subjects to remember as detailed as possible the specified objects in the museum and they are allowed to either simply watch or take pictures. The next day, those who took pictures of the subjects could recall fewer names of the items being shot and were less able to remember the details of them. "The reason may be this: at the moment we press the shutter, we hint that we're 'doing the right thing, and now it's time to do the next thing...', therefore, the brain will no longer be able to enhance the memory of some activities." Says by Linda Hankel, a psychology professor at the University of Fairfield.

3. Say "I" more often to show confidence

You may feel that people often speak with "I" are very confident. But some researchers at the University of Texas have recently done a study of classifying people's conversations and e-mails, finding that those who frequently use "I" are less confident than those who use the word less. "Pronouns like me, you and him reflect where our attention is focused." Says by researcher James Penny back, a professor of psychology at the University of Texas. People who like to use "I" pay attention to themselves, probably because of strong self-awareness, sense of insecurity, or eagerness to get others' affection. On the contrary, those who are confident use more frequently is the word "you", as they put most of the attention to the outside world, and hope for getting positive feedback.

4. 痴迷于健康饮食

研究者们最近通过对五十项研究进行分析发现，对"吃什么好"思考太多，会干扰你达到目标。荷兰乌得勒支大学心理学研究者杰西·胡伯兹认为，我们的选择越多，就越有可能偏离自己的目标。"如果一个人过多地关注自己以后的饮食和健康，可能会对此时的饮食习惯产生干扰。"杰西说。"比如，一个人如果打算晚些时候去健身房，可能就会因为没时间做饭而吃一些垃圾食品。"那么应当怎么办？养成一个你可以轻松实行的良好生活习惯，比如每天早上吃同一种健康早餐，或者下班后步行回家，把好习惯坚持下去，就不必因为考虑太多而分心。

5. 活在当下

传统智慧告诉我们：你不应该留恋过去。但是，英国南安普顿大学的最近一项研究发现，对很久以前的事情有恋旧情结，能够增长一个人对未来的自信。那么，过去和未来在我们的脑海里有着怎样的联系呢？研究者解释说，念旧记忆让我们自己对他人的亲密感更深。念旧记忆可以扩展我们的社交联系，从而增强自信，让我们能更加乐观、自信地生活。打个比方，如果你回忆起了上中学时和同学手拉手溜冰时的快乐，你便会对过去的生活有种满足感，从而对现在的自己感觉更好，并且对未来更有信心。

6. 灯光越暗越浪漫

如果你想暗下灯光，以此来增加浪漫气氛，或者增强你的吸引力，那你可能就会浪费一个晚上的大好时光了。加拿大多伦多西北大学的科学家们最近研究发现，开亮灯光可以使任何一种氛围和所有的情绪都得以强化，包括积极的和消极的。研究者安排了一组人参与了一系列测试，包括品尝从淡到浓的鸡翅酱汁的味道、听到从负面到正面的词语后

164

4. Obsession with a healthy diet

Researchers recently analyzed 50 studies and found that thinking too much about what to eat could interfere in your goals. Jesse Huberts, a psychology researcher at the University of Utrecht in the Netherlands, believes that the more choices we have, the more likely we are to deviate from our goals. "If a person pays too much attention to their future diet and health, it may interfere in the eating habits at this time." Jesse said. "For example, if a person intends to go to the gym later, he may eat some junk food because there is no time to cook." So what should you do? Develop a good lifestyle that you can easily implement, such as eating the same healthy breakfast every morning, or walking home after getting off work and sticking to good habits, without having too much worries about it.

5. Live in the moment

Traditional wisdom tells us: you should not be nostalgic for the past. But a recent study by the University of Southampton found that nostalgia for the past could increase one's confidence in the future. So, what is the link between the past and the future in our minds? Researchers explained that nostalgia makes our own sense of intimacy deeper. Nostalgia can expand our social connections, thereby increasing self-confidence, so that we can live more optimistically and confidently. For example, if you recall the joy when you were skating hand in hand with classmates in middle school, you will have a sense of satisfaction in the past life, feel better about yourself at present, and become more confident in the future.

6. The darker the lighting, the more romantic it is

If you want to darken the lights in order to increase the romantic atmosphere, or enhance your attraction, you may waste a good time for the evening. A recent study by scientists at Northwestern University in Toronto, Canada, found that lighting could strengthen any atmosphere and all emotions including positive and negative ones. The researchers arranged for a group of people to participate in a series of tests, from tasting the

的反应、评价几位女士的魅力等，而进行测试的屋子灯光一次为明亮、一次为昏暗。结果发现，在灯光较明亮的屋子里，人们的味觉更敏感、对词语的反应更强，人们在光线明亮的屋子里对女士们的评价也是更有魅力。其中的科学机制尚未研究清楚，但是多伦多大学研究者说，明亮的灯光可能会对我们的情绪系统产生刺激作用，因为我们会本能地感觉明亮意味着热量、热情，从而提高了我们的感受力。

7. 凡事顺其自然

现在很多人都推崇一种心理技能：认知重建，也就是重新评价我们对一件事物的看法，从而让我们获得更好的状态。在我们遇到自己难以预见结果的事情时，认知重建大有用武之地。不过，一项新研究发现，当人们遇到可以改变的情况时，再使用认知重建来搪塞，就会使我们更紧张和沮丧。美国兰卡斯特大学心理学教授艾里森·特洛伊认为，这是因为认知重建会阻碍一个人采取有效行动纠正出现的问题。想象一下，如果你的人际关系如日中天，部分原因是因为你的挥金如土。而通过认知重建，你可能会认为自己并没有做错什么，也就难以懂得花钱要量力而行的道理。而如果一个人无论错误大小都能给自己找到借口，则可能会造成积重难返的恶果。

载于《知识窗》

智 慧 箴 言

那些习以为常既已成形的生活经验，并不是为了固定这个世界从而形成规则，而是为我们提供了思考生活的切口，让我们有了辨别真伪的能力。勇于探索是对生活的热爱。

sauce of chicken wings, from light to thick, reaction after listening to the negative to positive words, evaluating the charm of several women. During the tests, the light in the test room was bright one time and dim the other. It was found that in a bright lit room, people were more sensitive to taste, more responsive to words, and they think women are more attractive tn bright room. The scientific mechanism has not yet been explored, but researchers at the University of Toronto say that bright lights may have a stimulant effect on our emotional system, because we instinctively feel that brightness means heat and enthusiasm, thus enhancing our ability to feel.

7. Everything comes naturally

Many people now admire a psychological skill: cognitive reconstruction, that is, to re-evaluate our view of a thing, so that we get better. Cognitive reconstruction is useful when we encounter things that are difficult to predict. However, a new study found that when people encounter situations that can be changed and use cognitive reconstruction to prevaricate, it will make us more nervous and frustrated. Lancaster University psychology professor Ellison Troy believes that this is because cognitive reconstruction will hinder a person to take effective actions to correct problems. You can image it this way, for example, if your relationships are on the rise, partly because you spend money like water. And through cognitive reconstruction, you may think you have not done anything wrong, and therefore it is difficult to know how to spend money properly. And if a person, regardless of the severity of the error, can find an excuse for himself all the time, it may give rise to a problem that is hardly resolved.

Being accustomed to life experience that have been accustomed to is not to fix the world to form the rules, but it gives us a way to think about life, so that we will have the ability to identify the authenticity. The courage to explore is the love of life.

撑死自己的蚊子

文 / 梅若雪

贪婪是许多祸事的原因。

——伊索

"人是一点灵魂载负着一具肉体","来自命运的东西并不脱离本性"。这是摘自《沉思录》一书的句子,该书中如这样朴实却直抵人心的句子非常多。

由《沉思录》中这样的句子想到了蚊子。

一直以来,人们皆以为当暴雨来临时,蚊子和蜻蜓、蝴蝶一样,躲藏在雨淋不着的地方。美国佐治亚州理工学院的一位叫乔治·库克的工程师对这一说法表示质疑,日前,他借助于高速摄影机,对暴雨中的蚊子进行了观察。果然,暴雨来临时,蚊子并不是藏起来,而是迎着暴雨自由地飞行。

雨滴落在蚊子的身上,它们为何一点也不在乎呢?通过进一步观察,得知雨滴之所以不能将它们砸翻,就在于雨滴的重量是蚊子的50倍。也就是说,因蚊子自身的质量轻,所以不能与雨滴形成猛烈的撞击。

A Mosquito that Die from Overeating

Greed is the cause of many calamities.

—— Aesop

"Man is a little soul carrying a flesh" "Things born of the fate are not divorced from nature". These sentences are taken from *Meditation*, a book filled with lost of simple but straightforward remarks.

These sentences also remind people of mosquito.

For all the time, people think that when the rain comes, mosquitoes, like dragonflies and butterflies will hide in places that cannot be soaked by rain. George Cook, an engineer of Georgia Institute of Technology, questioned this statement and a few days ago, he observed mosquitoes in heavy rain with high-speed cameras. It is obvious that when the rain comes, the mosquito is not hiding, but free to fly against the heavy rain

Why mosquitoes are not worried about raindrops on their body? With further observation, it is learnt that the reason why raindrops cannot throw them is that the weight of a raindrop is 50 times that of a mosquito. That is to say, the light weight of a mosquito cannot form a violent collision with raindrops.

However, after further observation, George, found that mosquitoes had been knocked down or struck by raindrops of rain, and it was the case when they just sucked blood. The volume of a mosquito will swell several times

169

不过，乔治在进一步观察之后，发现蚊子也有被雨滴撞翻甚或砸死的情况，这就是它们在刚刚吸了血的时候。一只蚊子吸了血后，体积会膨胀好几倍，如果再遇上沉重的雨滴时便会被砸得血肉横飞。蚊子的命运就这样被它的贪婪改变了。

　　蚊子究竟有多贪婪？在吸血时，被吸血的人如果将叮咬位置附近的肌肉收缩或拉伸，这时拔不出喙的蚊子会不停地吸下去，直至将自己撑死。

　　再回到《沉思录》。

　　我们知道，《沉思录》是由古罗马的一位皇帝——马可·奥勒留所写。这位皇帝在位的时候，战争频繁，瘟疫流行，甚或地震也频频来凑热闹，但不少历史学家仍将那个时期评定为适合人类居住的时代之一。

　　人们也许以为，这样的评价是得益于《沉思录》这本书。其实，奥勒留的德行不仅仅体现在脑海里与纸张上，而且在一举一动中也表现出了他的光明磊落和慈悲为怀。打起仗来，他总能身先士卒，在物质极度匮乏的时候，战士不吃，他绝不会先动刀叉；战士不饮，即使他渴得口中冒烟也会忍着。有人兵变夺位，在主谋被杀后，奥勒留只下令焚烧了兵变的所有材料，却不再追究参与叛乱的人。他还大力兴办慈善事业，让饱受战乱之苦的人得以温饱。

　　经过奥勒留的励精图治，国家终于得到振兴。

　　可谁也想不到，奥勒留去世后，继承皇位的康茂德，竟然是一个昏庸无道之人，一万多人被他残忍地杀害。比如，他让人与他角斗，自己手持利刃，却只允许对方拿着木棍之类的东西。而且哪怕是对方伤了他一点皮肤，他也要杀害对方的全家。每次角斗，他都让国家支出巨额费用，致使国力空前虚乏。

after they suck blood and will be smashed if it encounters a heavy raindrop. The fate of the mosquito was so changed by its greed.

How greedy is an mosquito? When it is sucking blood, if the person contracts or stretches the muscle near the bitten part, the beak of mosquitoes will not be pulled out so that the mosquito will continue to suck down until it dies.

Back to *Meditation*.

We know that *Meditation* was written by Marco Aurelius, an emperor of ancient Rome. When the emperor was on the throne, there were frequent wars, epidemic plagues, and even earthquakes. But many historians still rated it as one of suitable periods of human habitation.

People may think that such an evaluation is resulted from the book *Meditation*. In fact, Aureliu's virtue not only reflected in the mind and on the paper, and every move of him shows his openness and compassion. He always took the lead in a war. When there was a dearth of food, if warriors did not eat, he would never eat; if warrior did not drink, even if he was very thirsty, he would endure it. In rebellion, when the chief plotter was skilled, Aurelius ordered to burn all the materials related to the mutiny and no longer accused the followers in rebellion. He also vigorously set up charitable causes, so that people suffering from war could get enough food and clothing.

With Aurelius' good governance, the country was finally revitalized.

But no one could ever thought of the fact that when Aurelius died, Commodus, the man inherited the throne, a stupid person who cruelly killed more than 10,000 people. For example, he asked people to fight with him. But he could hold blade while the other one was only allowed to hold a stick and things like that. If the other man hurt his skin, he would kill his whole family. Every time the wrestling took place, he would let the state spend huge amounts of money, resulting in an unprecedented lack of national strength.

Commodus was assassinated by his follower after his ten years ruling, and the ancient Rome fell apart as a result, developing into the era of separatist melee and the golden age created by five virtuous Emperors had long gone.

康茂德在执政十多年后被属下暗杀，古罗马从此分崩离析，进入割据混战时代，五贤帝开创的黄金时代一去不复返了。

也许有人会说，这是康茂德自作孽，其实，这也是他的父亲奥勒留留下的祸根。古罗马实行的是"禅让"制，奥勒留的皇位就是由安东尼"禅让"给他的。他却破坏了"传贤不传儿"这一美好传统，将皇位传给了儿子康茂德。

两千多年后，《沉思录》依然被视作哲学经典，影响着千千万万的人，甚或许多国家的一代又一代领导人。但奥勒留这位"近于完美"的皇帝，在选择继承人上，却让私欲占了上风，致使儿子康茂德嗜血成性，不惜一切来满足自己的贪欲，不仅使得康茂德被历史所唾弃，也危害了国家与人民。

奥勒留这段历史，给人这样一种警示：一个人心灵的强大毕竟是有限的，纵使如奥勒留这样具有"文韬武略、宅心仁厚"的人，倘要让世界上少一些"撑死"自己的"蚊子"，必须得依靠健全的法律与制度，并辅之以完善的教育。只有这样，才能让更多的灵魂真正地"轻"起来……

载于《思维与智慧》

智 慧 箴 言

生活，是追求在心路上，被走成欲望；人生，是磨难在枝头上，被晾晒成了坚强。背上行囊，就会负累；放下包袱，就会快乐，无论走过多少坎坷，简单的日子总有快乐。一方陋室，亦能心境自如；一壶淡茶，仍品恬淡生香。

Some people may say that this is the fault of Commodus himself. In fact, this is the cause of his father. Ancient Rome adopted the abdication system and the throne of Aurelius was abdicated by Anthony. But he destroyed the great tradition that "the throne should be delivered to those responsibilities and capabilities instead of emperor's sons" and gave the throne to his son Commodus.

More than two thousand years later, *Meditation* is still regarded as a philosophical classics, affecting thousands of people, and even generations of leaders in many countries. However, the "near perfect" emperor allows his personal desires to take lead in the choices of heirs, resulting in a bloodthirsty son Commodus who would do everything to meet his own greed. This not only made Commodus rejected and disdained by history, but also endangered the country and the people.

This history of Aurelius gives such a warning: a person's strong mind, after all, is limited, even it is a kind people who is proficient both in literary and military strategies like Aurelius. If we want to make the world with fewer "mosquitoes" that "overeating to death", we must rely on sound laws and systems supplemented by comprehensive education. This is the only way to make more souls really "light" up…

Life is the pursuit in mind, which may be turned into a desire; life is suffering in branches, which can be dried into strength. Backpack will become a burden; while put down the burden, it will be happier. No matter how rough the road is, a simple life is always happy. A shabby room can also create a carefree mind; a pot of weak tea can still fill life with fragrance.

每次只追前一名

文 / 春秋

人生中最重要的不是位置，而是前进的方向。

——冯宇学

一个女孩，小的时候由于身体纤弱，每次体育课跑步都落在最后。这让好胜心极强的她感到非常沮丧，甚至害怕上体育课。这时，女孩的妈妈安慰她："没关系的，你年龄最小，可以跑在最后。不过，孩子你记住，下一次你的目标就是：只追前一名。"

小女孩点了点头，记住了妈妈的话，再跑步时，她就奋力追赶她前面的同学。结果从倒数第一名，到倒数第二名、第三名、第四名……一个学期还没结束，她的跑步成绩已到中游水平，而且也慢慢地喜欢上了体育课。

接下来，妈妈把"只追前一名"的理念引申到她的学习中。"如果每次考试都超过一个同学的话，那你就非常了不起啦！"

就这样，在妈妈这种理念的引导教育下，这个女孩 2001 年居然从北京大学毕业，并被哈佛大学以全额奖学金录取，成为当年哈佛教育学院录取的唯一一位中国应届本科毕业生。她就是朱成。

之后，朱成在哈佛攻读硕士学位、博士学位。读博期间，她当选为有 11 个研究生院、1.3 万名研究生的哈佛大学研究生总会主席。这是

Set a Small Goal Each Time Like Outrunning the One Before You

The most important thing in life is not where you are but which way you are going.

——Feng Yuxue

A girl was once thin and weak in her childhood, and as a result, was always the last one in races at P.E. She was depressed and afraid to take P.E. classes. Every at this time her mother would comfort her, she said, "you are the youngest one in your class. So it doesn't matter to be the last one. But remember, next time all you need is to outrank the one in front of you."

The little girl nodded and remember mother's words by heart. When it came to another race, she tried her best to outrank the one in front of her. Before the end of the semester, her ranking in races were top 50% from the last, last but one, last but two, last but three, last but four… And she became interested in P. E.

More than just race, her mother guided her to apply the theory to academic study. "It will be extraordinary if you can outrank the one in front of you in every exam."

Under the guidance of this theory, the girl, graduated from Peking University, was offered a full scholarship and became the only Chinese undergraduate admitted to Harvard University at graduating year. Her name is Zhu Cheng.

Zhu Cheng was granted master's and doctor's degree at Harvard. In her doctoral study, she was elected the chairwoman of Postgraduate

哈佛 370 年历史上第一位中国籍学生出任该职位，引起了巨大轰动。

希华·莱德是英国知名作家兼战地记者，第二次世界大战结束后，他谋到了一个写广告剧本的差事。出于信任，广告商并没有跟他签订什么合同，也没有明确规定他一共需要写多少个剧本。平心静气的莱德一直不停地写，竟然一口气完成了 2000 个广告剧本，这个成绩令世人震惊，甚至连他自己都感到十分意外。而如果当初广告商要与他签订合同的话，别说是 2000 个剧本，就是 1000 个，他也会退避三舍。

世界著名撑竿跳高运动员布勃卡有个绰号叫"一厘米王"，因为在一些重大的国际比赛中，他几乎每次都能刷新自己保持的纪录，将成绩提高一厘米。当成功地跃过 6.15 米、第 35 次刷新世界纪录时，他不无感慨地说："如果我当初就把训练目标定在 6.15 米，没准儿会被这个目标吓倒。"

把目标降低到"一厘米"，把期望缩小到"一个剧本"，分时限、分阶段去实现人生的抱负。让孩子放下包袱，轻装上阵，集中精力做好今天，做好当前，继而稳扎稳打，满怀信心地走向明天，走向未来。

"只追前一名"，就是所谓的"够一够，摘桃子"。没有目标便失去了方向，没有期望便失去了动力。但是，目标太高、期望太大的结果，不是力不从心，便是半途而废。明确而又可行的目标，真实而又适度的期望，才能引领人脚踏实地，胸有成竹地朝前走。

"只追前一名"，是一种人生的跨越，不仅需要智慧，更需要胆识。

载于《少年天地》

智慧箴言

> 许多人在做事的时候，喜欢列一个庞大的计划，写下不切合实际，并且超越了自己的能力范围的目标，最后不得不愤愤放弃。这给我们一种启示，只追赶离你最近的目标，一步步超越，这样你才会走得更远。

Student Union out of 13,000 students from 11 departments. In the course of Harvard's 370-year history, she was the first Chinese student to be elected.

Siward Ryde is a well-known author and war journalist from the UK. In past-WWII period, he got a job as an advertisement script editor. His employer never signed an agreement with him or came to an deal concerning how many scripts he should write due to his trustworthiness. Even himself was surprised Without any pressure, he made astonishing work by writing 2,000 scripts. If he signed agreement with his employer, he might not be able to write 1,000 scripts, let alone 2,000, and might even decline the job offer.

Bubka, a world-famous pole vaulter, gains a nickname, "One Centimeter King", because in major international competitions, he broke his own record each time by 1 centimeter. When he made it to 6.15 meters, the 35th time he broke his record, he couldn't help saying, "If I set my objective as 6.15 meters in the first place, I might discourage myself. "

Reduce your ambition into minor goals, one centimeter or one script, set a timeline of minor goals and realize each in respective time period. Let the children put down the burden and travel light. Help them walk to the future confidently.

Catch up the one in front of you as your goal is like picking the peaches from your closest reach. Without goal, one will lose bearing and without expectation, one will lose passion. However, set goals too high or expect too much might result in self doubt and giving up halfway. Clearly and wisely set goals can guide you to success step by step.

Only catching up with the previous one, is a kind of life span. It needs both wisdom and boldness.

Many people are prior to making ambitious plans and unrealistic goals which can be out of heir capacity. In the end, many of them have to give up. It tells us that chasing only the nearest target, you'll go farther and farther step by step and get closer to success.

哈斯特鹰的悲剧

文 / 沈岳明

太强必折，太张必缺。

——《六韬》

小时候看武侠小说，里面有一些诸如孤独求败、武林盟主、东方不败等这样的称号，这些名字，都是天下无敌、唯我独尊的意思。

别说做到天下无敌是件不可能的事情，就算真正达到了天下无敌的境界，也未必就是一件好事。因为不管是武侠小说里，还是现实生活中，那些追求天下无敌的人，没有哪一个落得了好下场。

人类如此，其他动物也是一样。在新西兰南岛，曾经生活着一种鸟类，名叫哈斯特鹰，是当时陆地生态系统中"最高级"的掠食者，位于食物链的最顶端，完全算得上"天下无敌"了。

最大的哈斯特鹰重达18公斤，翼展长度达3米，站立起来达1.4米。它能以每小时高达80公里的速度捕食猎物。当然，其他动物，包括人类，也是它们的捕食对象。

由于没有天敌，而且食物丰富，哈斯特鹰任意进食，并让自己的身体疯长。身体越大，力量会更大，捕食也越多，进食则更多。如此循

The Tragedy of Haast's Eagle

If it is too hard, it will surely break; if it is too expended, it will certainly be defective.

——*Six Arts of War*

In fantasy novels are characters like the Flash, Iron Man, Spider Man, etc. who are all the embodiment of the invincible.

In fact, it's impossible to be invincible. But if one can, it might not be a good thing. Because whether in novels or in reality, life of the invincible doesn't have a happy ending.

It is the same theory when it comes to human and animals. In South Island of New Zealand, there once lived a kind of bird, Hasst's eagle, which was the prime predator in its territorial ecosystem. On top of the food chain, it's equal to the word invincible.

The largest Hasst's eagle weigh 18 kilograms. Fully extended, its wings can be 3 meters long, and standing up, it is 1.4 meters high. The speed of 80 kilometers per hour enabled it to prey on large animals, and also human.

With no natural predators and abundant food, the Hasst's eagle could always satisfy its appetite, and as a result, it grew larger and larger. The larger it was, the stronger it could be, the more games it got and the larger appetite it had. It's a vicious circle. In the end, it grew from a rather small

环，让它们的体重从最初不超过 1 公斤的小鹰，慢慢地达到原来的 15 倍，进食量自然也达到原来的 15 倍。

据新西兰《生物公共图书馆杂志》介绍，在 1500 年左右，哈斯特鹰便灭绝了。灭绝的原因，不是遭遇了天敌，而是因吃不饱而饿死的。在没有天敌的时候，自己便是自己的天敌。

对比哈斯特鹰的"兄弟"们，我们现在依然能看到它们的身影，听到它们的叫声。它们的个子不大，但灵巧异常，尽管它们的名字稍有不同：老鹰、雕、鸢等，但在一百多万年前，它们与哈斯特鹰同属鹰类。

载于《青年博览》

智慧箴言

物竞天择，适者生存。有些东西注定是要消亡的，正所谓盛极必衰。

eagle less than 1 kilogram to a big one 15 times larger than its former figure and also 15 times more than its former appetite.

According to *Public Library of Bioinformatics*, in 1500s, the Hasst't eagle died out. The reason was not for predators but for starving to death. When there were no predators, the Hasst's were their own predators.

Now we can still see relative species of the Hasst's eagle and see their figure. They are not big but very agile. They may have different names such as eagle, vulture, glede, etc. But more than a million years ago, they all belonged to accipiter.

The fittest survive in natural selection. Like the saying goes, in its heyday comes falling, some species are destined to extinction.

生命在于"静止"

文 / 张珠容

耐得住寂寞，才能争得到繁华。

——佚名

在澳大利亚，有一些动物具有逃避时间的能力。夏季，围巾蜥蜴会在食物不足的时候进入半休眠状态，来逃避难熬的时光，此时，它们新陈代谢的速率只有正常状态下的三分之二。这个状态下的围巾蜥蜴每周只进食一次，因此只需花很少的时间去觅食。但这并不意味它们不会碰上天敌，黑鸢就常常盯着它们。

为了逃脱猎食者的捕杀，蜥蜴会迅速将自己切换到安全状态。它会出人意料地奔跑，然后以惊人的速度跳到最近的一棵大树上。大树是它安全的避难所，无论是对付猎食者，还是太阳的高温，都是如此。躲到树上之后，围巾蜥蜴又迅速恢复到半休眠状态，它只对太阳的移动做出反应，保持自己始终处于树荫之下。依靠假死状态，围巾蜥蜴度过了整个夏天。

动物界还有状态更深的假死，那就是将休眠状态的身体冰冻起来。凌蛙会在冰雪到来时进入冬眠状态，冰对一般的动物都是致命的，这种蛙也不例外。但是凌蛙可以在每个细胞内分泌葡萄糖，这些葡萄糖正是天然的防冻剂，能保护凌蛙的重要器官。同样，在冬天的时候，北美洲

Life Lies in "Stillness"

Endure the loneliness before you enjoy the prosperity.

——Anony

In Australia, some animals have the ability to get away from time. In summer, the scarf lizards would be in a semi-dormant state with food scarcity to escape the tough time. During that time, their metabolic rate is only two-thirds of the normal state. Scarf lizards in this state only eat once a week, so it takes little time to find food. But it does not mean that there are no predators, in fact, black kites are often looking for them.

In order to escape the hunting of predators, the lizards will quickly switch to a safe state of their own. They will run unexpectedly, and jump to a nearest tree at an amazing speed. Trees are shelters, either against predators, or to escape from the sun heat. After hiding in the tree, scarf lizards quickly return to the semi-dormant state again, and only respond to the movement of the sun, assuring them under the shade. Relying on suspended animation, scarf lizards spend the entire summer safely.

There is a deeper state of suspended animation among animals, that is, to freeze the dormant body. Ling frogs will start to hibernate when the snow and ice come. Ice is deadly to the animals, and the frog is no exception. But ling frogs can secre to glucose in each cell. The glucose is natural antifreeze, which can protect the important organs of the frogs. Likewise, in winter, half of North American turtles' bodies are frozen, and

小井龟一半的身体组织也被冻结起来，它们也在深度冰冻的状态下度过冬天。这两种动物处在假死状态的时候，心脏会停止跳动，就像是真的死了一样。到春天冰雪融化的时候，凌蛙和小井龟就复活了。它们的解冻顺序都是从内到外，先是心脏，然后是身体。一旦解冻，这些动物就会迅速利用仅有的几个月的活动时间。

对于哺乳动物来说，生命的长短和身体的大小也是成正比的。象鼩很少能活过两岁，而大象则可以活过60岁，但是在生活的步调上，大象比象鼩要慢上30倍。大象的心跳每分钟只有25下，而象鼩的心跳则可以达到每分钟800下。在如此不同的生命速率下，它们很难意识到对方的存在，或者说，很难意识到对方的动作结果是什么。象鼩不仅以比大象快30倍的速度度过它自己的日子，而且它的身体老化进程也同样在加速。看起来，大个头的迟缓动物比小个头的敏捷动物有着更长的寿命，但实际上，它们却有着近乎同样的心跳总次数——心脏在跳动8亿次以后，大多数动物都会死去。

当然，捕食者也会在寿命极限到达之前提前倒下。处于食物链顶端的食肉动物唯一面临的威胁，就是随年龄增长所带来的身体压力。肌体的不断劳损和修复会渐渐要了它们的命，毕竟肌肉只能被修复一定的次数，而不是无限。举例来说，一只年迈的狮子在捕食一头斑马时，斑马的反抗和逃跑会在无形中会损伤狮子的身体。所以，在不必要的情况下，狮子是绝不会奔跑的。

我们常说，生命在于运动，但围巾蜥蜴、凌蛙、小井龟、大象、狮子等动物却在静止中保护住了自己的体能储备，从而活得更长久。它们的生活方式告诉我们，在等待中积蓄力量，也是一种生存智慧。

载于《知识窗》

智 慧 箴 言

　　等待是生活的哲学，那些非洲草原上的霸主，无一不是在等待中积蓄力量，等待机会。这样才能厚积薄发，一招制敌。

they also spend winter in deep frozen condition. When the two animals are in suspended animation state, their heart will stop beating, like it's really dead. When spring comes and the snow and ice melts, ling frogs and small turtles resurge. Their thawing order is from inside to outside, first the heart, then the body. Once thawed, these animals will take advantage of only a few months of activity they have.

For mammals, the life span and the size of the body are proportional. A shrew's life is no more than two years while an elephant can live for over 60 years. But for the pace of life, elephants are 30 times slower than shrews. The elephant's heartbeats is only 25 times per minute, while a shrew's heartbeats can reach 800 times per minute. At such different rates of life, it is very difficult for them to realize the existence of each other, or what the results of others' actions are. As the shrew lives a life that is 30 times the speed of the elephant, its aging process is also accelerating. It seems that the big, slow animals have a longer life span than the smaller animals, but in fact they have nearly the same total number of heartbeats— most of the animals die after 800 million times of heartbeats.

Of course, predators sometimes die before their lives expire. The only threat to carnivores at the top of the food chain is the physical stress that comes with age. The body's constant strain and repair will gradually take their lives. After all, the muscle can only be repaired a certain number of times, not infinite. For example, when an aged lion preys on a zebra, the zebra's rebellion and fight could harms the lion's body. Therefore, the lion will never run unnecessarily.

People often say that life is movement, but scarf lizards, ling frogs, small turtles, elephants, lions and other animals are in the protection of their physical inanimation, thus living longer. Their way of life tells us that accumulating strength through waiting is the wisdom for survival.

Waiting is the philosophy of life, as those overlords on the African grassland both are waiting for accumulating energy and opportunities. One can accumulate energy richly and defeat enemy with one move.

别埋掉比豪车更宝贵的东西

文 / 宝谷

真正的慈善是神灵培植的作物。

——威·柯珀

2013 年 9 月中旬，巴西圣保罗市年逾花甲的富豪斯卡帕在各大报纸的头版刊登出这样的广告：本人将于 9 月 20 日把价值 150 万巴西雷亚尔的宾利车埋在自家后院。此消息一出，人们一片哗然，纷纷斥责斯卡帕："好好的车，为什么要平白埋掉它？这是极大的浪费！""如果你用不着这辆车，完全可以捐出去！"

2013 年 9 月 20 日，斯卡帕的车葬如期举行，媒体跟进、观众围观，好不热闹。车葬开始了，斯卡帕的司机开着宾利豪车缓缓驶入后院的墓穴。就在司机准备将车子开进墓穴的时候，斯卡帕大声喊道："停！在宾利下葬之前，我有事情要宣布！"

说完，斯卡帕朝现场所有人深深鞠了一躬，说："我首先向大家道歉，因为我欺骗了你们。今天，我在这里上演一场葬车的闹剧，只是想呼吁大家去注意一下，我们身边有多少人因为器官不足而死去？又有多少人带着健全的器官死去？"斯卡帕说完举起了一个"我是一名器官捐

Don't Bury Things Worthier than a Luxury Car

True charity is a crop cultivated by Good.

——William Cowper

Someday in the middle of September 2013, rich man Scarpa in his 60s, from Sao Paulo, Brazil, advertised on the front page of the newspapers: I am going to bury my $1.5 million Bentley in my backyard on September 20th. After the news was released, people threw fierce criticism on him, "Why are you burying it? It's such a waste!" "You can donate it if you don't use it!"

On September 20th 2013, the burial was held as scheduled. The media followed up and the audience watched, Scarpa's driver slowly drove the Bentley to the backyard. At the moment the driver was driving into the grave, Scarpa shouted, "Wait! Before it's buried, I have something to announce!"

Then he bowed to the people, and said, "I should apologize that I lied to you. Today, I arrange this farce just because I want to call your attention. How many people died because of lack of organs? And how many people died with healthy organs?" He put up a sign with "I AM AN ORGAN DONATOR. YOU?" on it.

All the people were stunned. As Scarpa explained, they finally understood the truth behind the car burial. At first, Scarpa was

献者，你呢?"的牌子。

现场所有人都震惊了，在斯卡帕的解释下，大家才明白这次车葬背后另有真相。原来，以往斯卡帕对捐献器官造福别人的善事也是漠不关心的，但几个月前，他亲眼目睹一个女孩因心脏衰竭而去世。医生说，如果给女孩移植一颗心脏，那么她就会继续活下去的，但愿意捐献心脏的人太少了，找不到合适的心脏。斯卡帕听完后难过极了。

就在这时，巴西器官捐赠机构准备策划"全国器官捐献周"活动，他们找到了斯卡帕，希望他在资金上予以资助。斯卡帕感慨良多，不仅捐了款、允诺死后可以捐赠自己可用的器官，还希望参与器官捐献周的策划和宣传。于是，机构借助斯卡帕的影响力，策划了这场别出心裁的器官捐赠宣传活动。

斯卡帕的善心果然感染了很多人。在他家的后院，人群开始骚动起来，不少人当场决定加入器官捐献者的行列。

实际上，斯卡帕葬车的确留给人们很多的思考：我们大多数人极少选择埋葬豪车，却经常选择埋葬掉比车更宝贵的东西——心、肺、肾等各种健全的器官。豪车与器官相比，又算得了什么呢？

载于《杂文选刊·下半月》

智 慧 箴 言

献出自己的器官，让别人继续活着，这样，自己的生命就会一直延续下去。

indifferent to organ donation. But a couple of months early, he witnessed a girl's death of cardiac failure. Doctors said that if there was a heart transplanted to her, she could have survived. But a suitable heart was too difficult to find since there were few donators. Scarpa was so depressed hearing this.

At that time, Brazilian organ donation organization was planning a "National Organ Donation Week" event, they found Scarpa and hoped he would fund it. Scarpa feeling a lot, not only donated money promised to donate their organs are available, and after death also went to participate in planning and publicity week of organ donation. Therefore, the organization planed this car burial activity with the help and influence of Scarpa.

Scarpa's benevolence inspired a lot of people. In his backyard, the crowd started to stir up and some people decided to join organ donors on the spot.

Indeed, Scarpa's car burial left a lot for people to think about: no one ever chose to bury his car, but many of them buried what is more precious than a car—hearts, lungs, kidneys, and other healthy organs. Compared with human organs, what's the value of a luxury car?

Some people donate their organs to continue others' life. By doing so, his own life can continue too.

极致的安第斯蜂鸟

文 / 张云广

善良和谦虚是永远不会令人厌恶的两种品德。

——斯蒂文生

安第斯山脉纵贯南美洲的西部，南北绵延八千九百多公里，号称地球上最长的山脉。

和世界上许多高山一样，安第斯山脉的不少地方环境恶劣，特别是高海拔的地区，那里不仅空气稀薄，而且由于稀薄的空气很难留住白昼太阳辐射的热量，所以夜间温度都会降到一个很低的值。每一种在这里"混"的动植物都要面临着很大的生存考验，比如，在山脉草地上生长的一种叫作普椰的凤梨科植物；比如，和普椰有着密切关系的安第斯蜂鸟。

普椰的寿命可达数年之久，在普椰行将枯萎之前，它会释放几年来植株内积聚的生命活力怒放出花冠高达五米的大型花朵，以此来为下一轮的荣枯做准备。

普椰的花朵里充满了极具诱惑力的花蜜，然而，由于这里海拔太高空气密度小，含氧量低，再加上气候寒冷，不仅身体单薄的飞虫无法振翅到达，就连一般的飞鸟也不能鼓翼而来。在这一生只有一次的灿烂而宝贵的

Superb Andeans Hummingbirds

Kindness and modesty are two qualities that will never be disgusting.

——Stevenson

The Andes runs through the western part of South America, stretching north and south for more than 8,900 kilometers, known as the longest mountain range on Earth.

Like many other mountains of the world, many places of the Andes are in harsh conditions, especially in high altitude areas, where there is not only thin air, but due to the thin air, it is difficult to keep the day sun radiation heat. So the night temperature will drop to a very low degree. Each of the "mix" animals and plants here are faced with a great survival test, for example, a pineapple plant growing in the mountain called coconut; or Andean hummingbirds that has a close relationship with coconut.

The life of coconut can be up to several years, before the coconut wither, it will release the accumulated vitality by giving birth to a large flower with its corolla blooming up to five meters in order to prepare for the next round of growth.

Coconut flowers are full of very attractive nectar, however, due to high altitude, low air density, low oxygen content, coupled with the cold weather, not only the weak winged insects cannot reach, even general birds cannot fly here. During its only splendid and valuable flowering season in its life, the only real "reliable" pollinator that coconut wait is Andean

花期里，普椰等待的真正"靠谱"的传粉使者只有一个——安第斯蜂鸟。

于是，在白天准确捕获到花朵盛开信息的安第斯蜂鸟飞来了！

要知道，这种羽毛华美、形体可爱的小精灵已经在夜间靠以近乎冬眠的方式与滴水成冰式的无边酷寒进行了数个小时的抗争。它们靠降低自身新陈代谢的速度硬是把自己的体温由三十八摄氏度降到了十四摄氏度，这种对环境的超级适应能力在鸟类中特别是对新陈代谢速度可达人的五十倍的蜂鸟家族而言是十分神奇和罕见的。

值得一提的是，与其他地区和其他种类的蜂鸟采用的以消耗大量体力为代价的高频拍翅式的常规采蜜方法不同，安第斯蜂鸟练就了一项"绝活"，那就是可以攀附在普椰的花冠上采食花蜜。这一绝活无疑有效地降低了它们能量的消耗，节约了"工作"的成本，从而大大提升了安第斯蜂鸟对高寒环境的适应能力。

就是这样，凭着特别能抗寒、特别能飞行和"特别会采蜜"的高超本领，在蜜汁多多的普椰花冠上，安第斯蜂鸟"旁若无人"般尽情而安心地享用到了其他虫鸟难以得到的美味。

物竞天择，万物皆在"天"的挑选规则之下。安第斯蜂鸟的成功哲学启示我们，不要轻易地抱怨命运的不公，也不要动辄就慨叹竞争的激烈，如果自己的本事还没有像安第斯蜂鸟那样优秀到不可替代的话。

载于《意林 12+》

智 慧 箴 言

在自己的能力没有达到一定高度的时候，千万不要抱怨，不然最后吃亏的还是自己。自不量力只会自取灭亡。

hummingbird.

Thus, Andean hummingbirds come when it accurately capture the full bloom in the daytime!

You know, this lovely elf with beautiful feather has been fought with unimaginable chills for several hours by using a way similar to hibernation to wrestle with a temperature so low that a drip of water can be immediately changed into ice. They reduce the speed of their metabolism, threw his body temperature from 38 degrees Celsius down to 14 degrees Celsius. This ability to adapt to the environment is extremely surprising and rare in birds, especially in the hummingbird family, which has a metabolic rate of up to 50 times that of human.

It is worth mentioning that, different from other kinds of hummingbirds in other regions that use the conventional honey extraction method by flapping at a high frequency at the expense of the consumption of great energies, Andean hummingbirds have developed a "unique skill", that is, they can cling to the corolla of the coconut to intake nectar. This unique skill undoubtedly reduces the energy consumption, saving the "work" cost, which greatly enhances the adaptability of Andean hummingbirds to the cold environment.

In this way, with the superb ability to resit cold, long duration of flying and "proficiency in gathering honey." Andean hummingbirds can enjoy peacefully the delicacies that other birds or insects are unable to get on the corolla of coconut.

Under nature's selection, all things follow the selection rules of "nature". Andean hummingbirds' successful philosophy reveals that we should not easily complain about the fate of injustice, or frequently lament the fierce competition, unless your skill is as good as the Andean hummingbird is irreplaceable.

When your ability cannot reach a certain height, never complain. Otherwise, the one that suffers losses will be yourself. Inability to understand you ability will only drive you to a complete failure.

193

兔子的论文

文 / 庞启帆 编译

智慧是命运的征服者。

——玉外纳

这天早上，兔子在森林里溜达时碰到了他的死对头狐狸。"哈哈，这次终于让我逮着你了！"说完，狐狸朝着兔子扑了过去。

兔子闪到一边，笑嘻嘻地说道："狐狸先生，我正在写一篇《论兔子比狐狸强》的论文，你不妨先跟我回去看看我写的是否有道理。"

"胡说八道！自古以来都是狐狸比兔子强，你不信吗？我现在就马上证明给你看。"说完，狐狸张嘴就要去咬兔子。

"不用这么着急嘛！如果你看完我的论文后，觉得我是胡说八道，再吃我也不迟呀！"兔子镇定道。

"好，量你也逃不出我的手掌心。就算你说得天花乱坠，事实上你也不可能强过我们狐狸。"狐狸笑道，然后他就跟着兔子回家，从此，森林里再也没有动物看见过这只狐狸的身影。

又一天早上，兔子在森林里溜达时碰到了他的另一个死对头狼。"哈哈，小兔子，我正愁早餐没着落呢！"说完，狼张开了他的血盆大口。

Rabbit's Paper

Wisdom is the conqueror of destiny.

——Juvenal

One morning when the rabbit wandered in the forest, he encountered his rival the fox. "Haha, I finally catch you this time!" Then, the fox rushed toward the rabbit.

"Mr. Fox, I'm writing a paper entitled *Rabbits Are Better Than Foxes*. You might as well go back with me to see if I'm making a case for it." The rabbit said, laughing.

"Nonsense! Since the ancient times, foxes have is always been stronger than rabbits. Don't you believe? I'll immediately prove it." Then, the fox opened his mouth to bite the rabbit.

"No need to rush! If you read my paper and still feel it's nonsense, you can eat me then!" Rabbit answered calmly.

"Well, you cannot escape my palm anyway. Even if you put it hype, in fact, you cannot be stronger than us." Fox laughed, and then he followed the rabbit home. Since then, no animal has ever seen this fox in the forest.

On another morning when the rabbit strolled in the forest, he met another enemy the wolf. "Haha, a small rabbit, I was worried about my breakfast just now!" Then, the wolf opened his mouth.

"Wait, wait!" Said the rabbit calmly. "I am writing a paper on *Rabbit Is*

"等等，等等！"兔子镇定地说道，"狼先生，我正在写一篇《论兔子比狼强》的论文，我想让你先跟我回去看看我写的是否有道理。"

"放屁！谁不知道狼比兔子强！我无须看你的狗屁论文，现在我就证明给你看！"说完，狼朝着兔子扑了上去。

兔子闪到一边，笑嘻嘻地说道："狼先生，如果你觉得我的论文是在胡说八道，再吃我也不迟呀！反正在你眼里，我是逃不出你的手掌心的。"

狼哈哈大笑，说道："好，我就让你多活几分钟，我倒要看看你是怎么颠倒是非的。"然后，他就跟着兔子回家了，从此，森林里再也没有动物见过这只狼的身影。

某一天，一只青蛙无意中闯进了兔子的家。他看到了这一幕：一头狮子正趴在兔子的房间里呼呼大睡，狮子的两边各有一堆白骨。在狮子的旁边有一张桌子，桌子上有一台电脑。兔子正坐在电脑前写论文，论文的题目是《论兔子比狐狸和狼强》。

各位，明白了吧，论文的题目是什么并不重要，重要的是你的导师是谁。

载于《小小说选刊》

智 慧 箴 言

这实在是一种高明的生存手段，正所谓互相合作才能实现双赢。

Stronger Than A Wolf, Mr. Wolf, I want you to go back with me to see if I made sense."

"Nonsense! Everybody knows that a wolf is stronger than a rabbit! I do not need to see your shit papers, and now I'll show you! "Then, the wolf rushed toward the rabbit.

The rabbit flashed aside and said with a smile, "Mr. Wolf, if you think my paper is nonsense, it is not late to eat me! Anyway, in your eyes, I cannot escape from your palm."

The wolf laughed and said, "Okay, I'll let you live for a few more minutes, and I'll see how you are inverted." Then he followed the rabbit home, and no animal has ever seen this wolf in the forest.

One day, a frog accidentally broke into the rabbit's home. He saw this scene: a lion is lying in the rabbit's room, sleeping and on each side of the lion, there is a bunch of bones. Next to the lion is a table with a computer. The rabbit is sitting in front of the computer to write a paper, entitled "*The Rabbit Is Stronger Than The Fox and Wolf*".

So, ladies and gentlemen, do you understand now? It is not important what the topic is, what matters is who your mentor is.

This is really a sophisticated means of survival, win-win situation can only be realized through the so-called mutual cooperation.

没有私心的吊床鸟

文 / 程刚

> 一切使人团结的是善与美，一切使人分裂的是恶
> 与丑。
>
> ——列夫·托尔斯泰

南美哥伦比亚佛朗卡斯特森林中有一种小鸟，它不像其他鸟儿那样在树上筑巢，而是喜欢以群体搭建一座吊床的方式休息，因此，当地人管这种鸟叫吊床鸟。

吊床鸟像麻雀一般大小，嘴部有弯弯的钩子，尾巴末端是一个小圆环。每到晚上，它们便成群结队地栖居一起，先找到适于搭床的树，一列列排好队。第一排吊床鸟最多，它们先将自己尾巴上的圆环套在树丫杈上，然后，用嘴勾住第二排小鸟尾巴上的圆环，第二排小鸟再用嘴勾住第三排尾巴上的圆环……

就这样，一排又一排小鸟连环勾套，直到最后一排小鸟用嘴勾住另一个丫杈为止，吊床就搭建成功了。吊床一般长度有三米多，宽有二米。当吊床搭好以后，许多吊床鸟便躺在床上安然地休息。

有人不禁要问，这么大的一张吊床，至少需要近百只小鸟搭建，

Selfless Hammock Birds

All that unifies is goodness and beauty, and all
that divide man is evil and ugliness.

——Leo Tolstoy

There is a small bird in the Francaster Forest of Colombia, South America, which does not nest in trees like other birds, but rather rests in the form of a hammock in groups, so the locals call it hammock bird .

A hammock bird is like a sparrow in general size with a curved hook on its mouth and a small ring at the end of the tail. Every night, they will be in droves to dwelling together, find suitable tree for sleeping and then line up. The first row of hammocks has the most birds, and they first put the ring on their tails on the tree rafts, and then hook the rings on their tails of the second row of birds with their mouths; the second row of birds will then hook the rings on the third row of tails with their mouths.

In this way, rows of birds chain hook sets, until the last row of birds' mouths hook up to another branch and then they successfully build a hammock. Hammock generally have three meters in length, and two meters in width. When the hammock is set up, many hammock birds will lie in bed safely to take a rest.

Some people can not help asking, such a big hammock requires at least nearly a hundred birds to build so that other hammock birds can rest

然后其他吊床鸟才能到床上休息。是不是它们群体中有专门搭床的鸟呢？答案是否定的。

原来，吊床鸟在搭床前，首先有一只要大声鸣叫，此后不断有鸟聚集过来开始搭床，它们不分雌雄。不分老幼，谁先到谁先搭，碰上哪个群就在哪个群搭，等所有的床搭好后，没有参与搭床的鸟便随意在一个床上休息。等到第二天，依然是这样，谁先到谁先搭，所以，所有的鸟都有可能参与搭床，又都有可能在床上休息。没有完全坐享其成的，也没有完全卖苦力的。

吊床鸟为何搭床睡觉至今也没有科学定论，但它们谁来得早谁搭床，谁来得晚谁休息的共存模式确实值得人类思考。许多时候我们共处一个环境里，因为私心，总是为一些利益争来争去，吊床鸟的共生模式是不是值得我们学习借鉴呢？

载于《辽宁青年》

智 慧 箴 言

这世间最伟大的力量，莫过于团结的力量。

on it. Is there a specific group of birds responsible for it? The answer is negative.

Actually, before setting up the hammock, one bird has to sing loudly to attract birds that come together to build up the hammock. All the birds, regardless of gender, or age, will set up the bed in sequence. When the beds are set, those that do not participate in bet setting can rest randomly on one bed. Tomorrow, the same happens again so that all the birds may participate in the setting process or rest upon a bed. There is no full sit back and enjoy or completely selling coolies.

There is no scientific conclusion why hammock birds set up bed for rest, but the coexistence model that those come early make bed, and those come late take a rest is indeed worthy of human thinking. For most of the time, we live together in an common environment, because of our selfishness, we always fight for some interests, so is it worthy of learning from the symbiotic pattern of hammock birds?

The greatest power in the world is the power of solidarity.

抬起我们的头

文 / 嵇振颉

预防胜于治疗。

——狄更斯

公交、地铁车厢内出现了专注于手机、平板电脑屏幕的"低头一族"，这究竟是科技进步为人们带来的福利，还是时代带给我们的无奈？

在拥挤的地铁、公交车里，众多年轻一族都作"低头看屏幕"状。手机或平板电脑上的网页、视频、小游戏，让这些上班族找到了打发往返途中无聊时光的有效途径。他们关注的范围，仅限于屏幕那方小小的空间，至于周围有其他异动，很难引起他们的注意。时间就在屏幕不停地闪动中悄悄溜走，如同潺潺的流水静静地从他们身边流过。

低头族现象不仅止于流动的公共空间，更多地表现在"人坐在一起，而心却各在他处"。无论是工作会议、朋友聚会，甚至是恋人约会，许多人都会觉得和身边的人无话可讲，反而对网络上的信息更感兴趣。当人们没有继续交流下去的兴趣时，这样的会议、聚会、约会也就成为一种鸡肋和例行公事。

Raise Our Heads

Prevention is better than treatment.

——Dickens

In a bus or a subway compartments, there are a large number of people who focus on mobile phones and table screens. Is this the welfare brought by the progress of science and technology or the helplessness brought by the times?

Nowadays, in a crowded subway or bus, most young people are "staring at their screen". Webpages, videos and games in their phones or pads are an efficient way for the office workers to pass the boring time on the way between home and office. Their focus is limited to the small space on the screen, even there are other change around them that are hard to get their attention. Time passes by the flashing screen like the murmuring running water.

More than just in public places, phubbing is becoming more and more normal in gatherings, people sit together but the heart is everywhere. Whether it's a workshop meeting or a party, even a date, many people are found speechless with the others and focused more on the Internet. When people find no interest in exchanging ideas with each other, meetings, parties and dates become routine with little value.

低头族的产生，有着深刻的背景。城市化进程的加速，生活节奏越来越快，客观上造成私人时间碎片化。不少年轻人希望抓住这些零碎的时间，通过数字终端进行娱乐休闲，以此放松紧张的身心。上网浏览、玩游戏、看视频等，低头一族在页面的不停切换中玩得不亦乐乎、乐在其中。

我并没有贬低低头族的意味，一个不懂得休息的人，不会拥有一个幸福的人生。可是，这一动作习惯的弊端还真应该引起我们的重视。

首先，有研究说，每天长时间接触电视及电脑，脑部会受到海量信息的过度刺激，由此导致注意力不集中，这势必会影响一个人的工作和生活的效率。

其次，过分依赖手机、平板电脑，会造成人际关系的冷漠。人间的真情，绝不是冷冰冰的数字和符号可以替代的。亲情、友情、爱情，正是在面对面的沟通交流中才可以不断加深、升华，而不是面对闪烁的屏幕时就可以擦出火花的。低头族好像大海中的孤岛，只专注于自己的"一亩三分地"，而忽视了自己的社会责任。如果任由这样的现象发展，整个社会将成为一盘散沙，而我们极有可能又退回到"原子式"的状态。

最后，低头一族会带来健康上的隐患。清晨的朝阳、落日的余晖、蹒跚学步的孩童、饱经岁月的老人、小草上的露珠，这些都是上天对我们的恩赐。如果埋首于数字终端，那么我们就错失了让身心愉悦的机会。低头注视液晶屏幕时，大脑依然处在高度紧张的状态，这哪是放松？分明是一种异化的"工作模式"。长此以往，无论是生理上还是心理上，都很难摆脱亚健康的状态。

The emergence of the low headed family has a profound background. As urbanization picks up paces, so does people's life. As a result, long and consecutive personal time now breaks into short pieces. The younger generation wants to seize every moment to relax themselves from the fast-paced life and work through digital entertainment, such as searching the Internet, playing games, and watching videos, to which the younger generation are so addicted.

I don't mean to disparage the younger generation for he who knows the importance of entertainment or lives a happy life. However, we should attach more importance to this habit.

First, a study shows, our brain receive excessive information stimulus due to long term of watching TV or searching the Internet. Therefore, it may result in attention deficit and impact on efficiency of work and life.

Second, too much attention on phones and pads can cause disparity in social relationships. Attachments between people can't be substituted by figures and symbols. Love between family members, friends and couples grows deeper and deeper only through face-to-face interactions, it's not possible to wipe sparks when facing the screen. Pubber isolates the younger generation like a solo island in the sea that lives in their own world and forget about their social responsibility. With more and more people phubbing, social integrity can be undermined and human being may fall back to the era like independent atoms.

Last but not the least, phubbing may cause physical diseases. Sunrise in the morning, sunset in the evening, toddling kids, senior people going through vicissitudes of life, and dew on the grass are all nature's bestow. If we bury ourselves in the digital information, we will lose the opportunity to enjoy natural beauty. While we are staring at the LCD screen, our brain remains highly intensified. Is it relaxing that we want? No, it is another "work pattern" for our brain. In the long run, it will put both our body and mind in a sub-healthy condition.

如果数字终端被我们适度、合理地利用，它们将是我们获取信息、娱乐休闲的强大助手。反之，我们就将成为它们的"奴隶"，在紧张刺激的画面中渐渐迷失真实的自我。

抬起我们的头吧！身边有很多美好的事物，等待我们去发现、去欣赏。

载于《文苑》

智 慧 箴 言

一个小知识：研究表明，低头看手机时，颈椎所承受的压力是平常的三倍还要多，时间久了，颈椎病就会找上门来。所以，尽量减少对电子产品的依赖是很有必要的。

Wisely used, the digital information will be instrumental in information acquisition and entertainment. Otherwise, we may be enslaved and lost in intense and exciting graphics.

So lift up our head now! There are so many beautiful things surrounding us, waiting to be found out.

A little tip: studies show that when we are lowering our head to the phone, the pressure on cervical vertebra is more than 3 times of the normal pressure. A long time, cervical diseases may occur. So, it's necessary to curb the dependence upon electric products.

找个敌人做搭档

文/十三页

> 可持续竞争的唯一优势来自于超过竞争对手的创新能力。
>
> ——詹姆斯·莫尔斯

在埃及的奥博斯城，有一座鳄鱼神庙。公元前 450 年，古希腊历史学家希罗多德曾来过这里。当时，他发现一个奇怪的现象，大理石水池中的鳄鱼游出水面的时候总爱张着大嘴。即使是吃饱喝足后，鳄鱼也总爱这样。让他惊讶的是，居然有一种灰色的小鸟站在鳄鱼嘴边为它啄食剔牙，鳄鱼却视而不见，并不伤害它。

这种灰色的小鸟是"燕千鸟"，每当鳄鱼饱餐后，就会懒洋洋地躺在河边闭目养神。这时候，燕千鸟就会飞到它们身边，于是鳄鱼张开大嘴，让这种小鸟飞到嘴里来清洁牙齿，燕千鸟则会把鳄鱼牙缝里的水蛭、苍蝇等食物残屑一一啄去。在鳄鱼的"血盆大口"中啄食，会让鳄鱼感到很舒服，燕千鸟成了鳄鱼的"保健员"。

假如鳄鱼忘记了它的"保健员"闭起大嘴睡觉时，或者燕千鸟在鳄鱼嘴里待够了的时候，燕千鸟就用它的羽毛摩擦鳄鱼的上颚，鳄鱼立即就打哈欠，燕千鸟会趁此机会飞出。返回时，无论鳄鱼在哪里，燕千鸟

Find an Enemy Partner

The only sustainable competitive advantage comes from innovation that outplaces your competitors.

——James Morse

There was a crocodile temple in the city of Obes in Egypt where in 450 B.C. the Ancient Greek historian Herodotus once came here. At that time, he observed a strange phenomenon that the crocodiles opened their mouths widely when swimming out of the marble pool. They kept doing so even if they were satiate. To his suprise, there was a grey little bird standing in the crocodile's mouth and picking its teeth, while the crocodile just ignored it.

This kind of bird is called "crocodile bird". Every time when the crocodiles finish a meal, they would lay near the river lazily with eyes closed. Then the birds would fly around. The crocodiles open their mouths, deliberately let the birds fly into their mouth and clean their teeth; the birds will peck the leeches, flies and other food debris. Crocodiles are quite comfortable with the birds' services, which make the birds their "hygienists".

If the crocodiles forget their "hygienists" and start to sleep with their mouths closed, or when the birds stay long enough in the crocodile's mouth, these grey birds rub the crocodile's palate with their feather, and the crocodiles would yawn to let the birds out. These birds are always found where there are crocodiles. Sometimes the birds nest around the crocodile

都能找到。有时候，燕千鸟干脆就在鳄鱼栖居地营巢，好像在为鳄鱼站岗放哨。稍有风吹草动，它们就会一哄而散惊叫几声，向鳄鱼报警，鳄鱼得到报警信号后，便潜入水底避难。

在所有鸟兽都避开凶残的非洲鳄鱼时，燕千鸟却安然无恙。

无独有偶，在大西洋中有一种一生都在鱼的嘴里生活的虾，叫绿虾，而这种鱼是扁鱼。在鱼嘴里生活，听起来非常危险。但令人惊奇的是，扁鱼绝不会把绿虾吞进肚里，它不但不吃，还会好好地保护绿虾。白天它潜伏在绿虾周围，夜晚把绿虾含进嘴里让它留宿，是什么原因让扁鱼对绿虾如此厚爱呢？

原来绿虾在水中游动时，身体晃动的频率极高，绿虾以自己身体的晃动吸引来了其他的小鱼来捕食，而前来捕食的小鱼就成了扁鱼的食物，绿虾则成了扁鱼引诱食物的诱饵。久而久之，绿虾就成了扁鱼生活不可分离的一部分，扁鱼也成了绿虾遇到危险时的保护神。

燕千鸟与鳄鱼，绿虾与扁鱼在食物链中的关系有目共睹。可是，面对强大的天敌，它们却能够安然地共处一隅。不得不令人佩服它们独具智慧的选择——找个"敌人"做搭档。

其实，无论是生活中或是职场中，不管是做大事业抑或是做小买卖，找个优秀的"敌人"做搭档都是明智的，因为利用双方的优势，会更好地解决问题，也一定会取得意想不到的双赢效果。

载于《谈心》

智 慧 箴 言

　　合作可以实现双赢，这是人生很重要的一课。有时候个人的力量是渺小的，难以抵挡外界的冲击。联合其他人，团体的力量就变得强大了。

habitats as if to safeguard them. If there were any slight signs of trouble, the birds would break up in a hubbub and make birdcalls to alarm the crocodiles, and after the crocodiles get the signal they sneak into the water.

When all other birds and beasts are trying to avoid the African crocodiles, the crocodile birds are living around them safe and sound.

The similar thing happens in Atlantic where there is a kind of shrimp called green shrimp living its entire life in the mouth of the fish called slivery pomfret. It sounds quite dangerous to live in fish's mouth. What is surprising is that the fish never swallows the shrimps but carefully protects them, lurking around them in the daytime and keeping them shelter during the night. Why is the fish so caring about the shrimps then?

It turns out that as the green shrimps shake their body frequently, they attract many small fish for predation; however, the shrimps are actually act as baits because the small fish they attract eventually become prey of the slivery pomfret. A long time, green shrimps become an indispensable part in slivery pomfrets' life while the latter are protectors of the shrimps.

The relationship between crocodile birds and crocodiles, as well as green shrimps and slivery pomfrets in the food chain is quite obvious. However, when facing a formidable natural enemy, all of them can live peacefully. Their wise choice is impressive, that is—to find an "enemy" partner.

In fact, no matter in life or career, no matter doing big things or small business, it is always wise to find an excellent "enemy" as your partner because both sides can take advantage of the other and come up with better ways to solve the problem and gain unexpected win-win results.

Cooperation can bring mutual benefits, which is an important lesson in life. Sometimes individual's power is too tiny but a group can be stronger when united with others.

一部电影背后的人生

文 / 石顺江

高山流水，非知音不能听。

——文天祥

1987 年，编剧罗纳德·巴斯在盐湖城采风时发现一个名叫金·皮克的自闭症患者，该患者记忆力超强，能一字不漏地背诵至少 9000 本书的内容。罗纳德·巴斯就从其个性中汲取灵感，写出了一个剧本。他找到一家电影公司的老板寻求合作，老板看后对他说道："很好，但一定要找导演打磨好才可以。"

一位导演看过故事梗概后立马告诉他道："主要人物太少了，只有兄弟两人开车跨越全美国的对话，何况其中一位心智还有问题，连一点打斗、谋杀或性之类的情节也没有，即使做成后也不会有大的上座率。"

罗纳德·巴斯找到大名鼎鼎的斯皮尔伯格来执导，他最初考虑导演此片，但单调的人物情景让斯皮尔伯格选择了中途退出。

他垂头丧气地来到电影公司老板面前诉苦道："他们都说不行，看来是编不成电影了……"老板对他说："别灰心，相信我的看法，一定会找到识货的导演的。"

Life Beyond a Film

One's lofty dreams can only be appreciated by bosom friends.

——Wen Tianxiang

In 1987, writer Ronald Bass found an autism patient named Kim Peek in Salt Lake City. This autism had good memory and could recite at least 9,000 books without dropping a letter. Ronald Bass drew inspiration from his personality and created a script. He sought cooperation with a Film Company whose boss told him that it was a very good footage, but it needed skilled director.

A director immediately told him after reading the outline, "There are few main characters and it only involves dialogue of two brothers who drive across the U.S, let alone something wrong with one's mind, even no plot of a little fighting, murder or sex. Even it is made into a film, it can't attract many audiences."

Spielberg, a famous director, considered to direct this film at first, but later quitted because of the monotonous character scene.

The writer lost his spirits and complained to the boss of the Film Company, "They all deny the story and it seems there is little hope to make it into films..." The boss said to him, "Don't be discouraged, believe in me, you will find a right director who understands its value."

巴瑞·莫罗是他找到的第五位导演。莫罗看完小说后，感动得泪流满面，答应一定完成该剧本的执导，最终电影成功摄制完成。一经上映便风靡全球，并先后获得了奥斯卡金像奖等四项大奖。

　　这部电影就是《雨人》，这位老板就是索尼娱乐事业公司的总裁彼得·戈柏。

　　提起这部影片，戈柏说："拿到这个剧本我就觉得有市场，有些导演只是太急功近利，一个企求立刻能看到成功的人往往放弃得也越快。就好像一块丑陋的石头，肤浅的人只会不屑一顾，而只有智者才知道，经过一番雕琢打磨，璞玉终会大放异彩。"

载于《当代青年》

智 慧 箴 言

　　正所谓千里马常有，而伯乐不常有。一个作品或者是人才，需得碰到真正赏识他的人才能展现他的全部意义。

Barry Morrow was the fifth director he referred to. Morrow was moved to tears after finishing the novel and promised to complete the direction of this script. Finally, the film was produced successfully and swept the world after put on the screen, also, it won four awards successively such as the Oscar Awards.

The movie is the *Rain Man*, and the boss is Peter Gober, President of SONY's Entertainment Company .

Mentioning the film, Gober said, "When I get the script, I feel there is a market. Some directors are eager for quick success and instant benefits and one that desires success immediately tends to give it up quickly. Like an ugly stone, shallow men will not spare a glance for it while wise men believe firmly that jade will shine once it is polished."

It is said that there are always talents but those who can discover the talents are rare. A good work or a talent should meet those that can really recognize them to realize its significance.